MW01173643

RESTORE
THE ROAD
HOME

ENCOURAGEMENT FOR
PARENTS OF PRODIGALS

JEFF **&** DIANA SEAMAN

ISBN: 979-8-89109-982-1 (paperback)
ISBN: 979-8-89109-984-5 (hardcover)
ISBN: 979-8-89109-983-8 (ebook)

This book is dedicated to our very first Battle Cry group. We came together in mutual pain, gave each other hope and received strength and encouragement from our Savior. Our prayer is that everyone who picks up a copy of this book will find friends like you.

CONTENTS

FOREWORD

"I don't want to go to church." This was the beginning of a spiritual downfall for our daughter. She was a teenager in her senior year of high school when she uttered the words I never thought I would hear her say. We're pastors, believers, and Christ followers who had diligently worked to keep our family focused on Jesus. However, with all of these advantages, she didn't want to follow the Lord. This left my wife and I feeling like failures. Where did we go wrong? What could we have done differently? Was there something we missed in her upbringing? All these questions were floating through our minds, and the enemy had his way in making us feel like hypocrites. As pastors we teach about "raising our children in the ways of the Lord," but we couldn't do it ourselves. The heartache was devastating, and nothing we did or said seemed to make a difference in our daughter's heart.

Unfortunately, there are thousands of God-honoring parents who find themselves in the same situation. They have done everything they know to do, but their prodigal has failed to come home. In Luke 15 we find the popular parable that Jesus shared about the story of the prodigal. The young son decided he wanted nothing to do with his father's plan for his life and embarked on a journey of spending his inheritance on foolish living. After he loses all his money, he realizes that his father's servants are now living better than he is living. He makes a decision to go home in the hope that his father will allow him to be one of the servants. As he makes his way down the road toward his father's estate, he turns the corner and enters the path that will lead him home. Unexpectedly, he finds his father standing on the path waiting for him. We don't know how long it took for his child to come home, but we do know the father had to wait. He most likely spent his time praying, believing, and hanging on to hope, trusting that God would turn his boy back to him . . . and he did! It didn't happen overnight, but eventually God turned it around for him.

My close friends, authors Jeff and Diana Seaman, address this topic head-on in their book *Restore the Road Home*. Filled with authenticity and transparency, they share the story of their own child who has walked away from the Lord after being raised in a Christ-centered home. They unashamedly share the guilt and pain they felt watching their child walk away from the mountain of faith they had built their life and family upon. The book includes the heartfelt stories of parents who have suffered the often lonely journey of waiting for a prodigal child to return to their faith. These real-life stories give us hope and remind us that God is still at work within the lives of our children. Jeff and Diana address the true and often unspoken emotions of those who are parents of a prodigal. The guilt, shame, loneliness, isolation, and heartache are all brought to light but are wrapped in a joyful hope that the victory can still be won. *Restore the Road Home* not only identifies the emotions of a prodigal parent, but it also provides practical application to help guide you throughout the journey you face.

I mentioned earlier that our daughter was a prodigal. When she graduated from high school, she floundered through community college and a part-time job. One day she joined us at church, and during the worship she leaned over and said, "I think God wants me to go to Hillsong Bible College in Australia." My wife and I were shocked. We had no idea where this was coming from, but we were going to do all we could to encourage her to follow through with what she was feeling. Three months later she was on a plane to Australia. After a couple months there, she was selected to sing with the worship team during one of their conferences. When the day of the conference arrived, my wife and I went online to watch the worship session. The band played four songs, and the camera angles kept going from the crowd, to the lead singer, to the guitar player, and back to the crowd. We were hoping to see our daughter, but they kept showing the same shots. Finally, on the last chorus of the last song, the camera zoomed in on our daughter and there she was, eyes closed, hands lifted, and praising our Savior with all her might. My wife and I stood in front of our laptop and just wept. Our prayer was finally answered . . . our prodigal had come home. Please hear me when I tell you, if He did it for us He can do it for you. Hang in there! Don't give up! Stay strong! Just when you think that all hope is gone, take a glance out your window and look down the dusty road . . . your prodigal is coming home.

Pastor Chris Sonksen

INTRODUCTION

The entire world recently learned what a global pandemic feels like. We went through many emotions as we watched things unfold that we seemed to have no power over. There was death, frustration, sickness, confusion, isolation, and fear. We all collectively hope to never go through that again.

Unfortunately, we believe we are still in the midst of a pandemic—a spiritual one. If you follow the research, you are aware that people are leaving their faith in Christ in droves. Even if you don't look at the official data, all you have to do is look around our churches. Yes, there are still beautiful, vibrant, Spirit-filled churches preaching the Word and lifting high the name of Jesus. However, there are people missing. People who have decided they are done following Jesus. Young people who have grown up in our children's churches and youth groups who are no longer serving the Lord. We would call these people "prodigals."

After the children of Israel entered the promised land, a new generation arose. A generation who had been born in the loveliness of the promises of God. They were never slaves in Egypt. They did not see the parting of the Red Sea. They never had to rely on manna to eat. They were not burdened with the experience of wandering in the desert for forty years or fighting the battles to take the land. Judges 2 describes the situation.

After Joshua had dismissed the Israelites, they went to take possession of the land, each to their own inheritance. The people served the Lord throughout the lifetime of Joshua and of the elders who outlived him and who had seen all the great things the Lord had done for Israel. . . . After that whole generation had been gathered to their ancestors, another generation grew up who knew neither the Lord nor what He had done for Israel. Then the Israelites did evil in the eyes of the Lord and served the Baals. They forsook the Lord, the God of their ancestors, who had brought them out of Egypt. They followed and worshiped various gods of the peoples around them. (Judges 2:6–7,10–12)

There is a popular saying in evangelicalism, "There are no grandchildren in heaven, only children." Meaning, no one is saved because they grew up in a Christian family. Our salvation does not transfer down to our children. Each person has to answer the call of the Holy Spirit to come to salvation through Jesus Christ on their own. Not always, but sometimes, that means they have to experience slavery, wander in the desert, or end up in the pigpen to come to their senses.

For those of us who have children who have walked away from the faith they were raised in, are we hopeless? Are our hands tied? Is there nothing that can be done? Absolutely not! In this book we want to bring you hope and a strategy to go to battle for your child. You may be waiting to see your child come back home, but you don't have to wait idly.

A few years ago we gave our son a book to read. We believed the book had some really valuable truths in it but were a little concerned that it could lend itself toward legalism. We told him to remember as he read that the book we gave him was not the Bible and its author was not Jesus. In other words, both the book and the author would have flaws and imperfections. That's a good thing to remember with any book you pick up, including this one.

The goal of any Christian book, author, preacher, sermon, etc. is not to never mess up but to always point you to the one who doesn't. Your authors are fallible and we will stumble sometimes. Your Savior is without blemish, and you can safely follow everything in His Word.

However, you can be confident in this: We are growing. Yes, we've been knocked down by the pain of a child rejecting our Savior. Where we once would spend days in despair, now we get back up pretty quickly. There was a time when we just observed the damaging work of the enemy. Now we fight back.

One final note before we continue. We will not be naming our child who is not serving the Lord and will be limiting the personal information we give about them while still hopefully relaying enough to share our story with you. This is our story. Maybe someday our child will write their own. We will be telling other stories of families we know and allowing them to share in their own words but will change their names and details as well.

Have you been sucker punched by your child's words, choices, or actions? Do you feel knocked down? We invite you to follow us through these pages. We won't promise that we'll never trip or stumble, but we will promise to lead you in the right direction. But the thing we want you to walk away from this book knowing in your bones is that you are not alone. So as we begin, let's take a look at how we got here.

CHAPTER 1

OUR STORY

The two of us grew up in very different households. I (Jeff) grew up in a home of drugs, alcohol, neglect, divorce, and every type of abuse. However, as I look back I can see God's gracious hand of protection and redemption upon me through it all. My dad moved with the construction jobs he could get, and when I was eleven years old that meant a move to the Sacramento area. The neighbors must have contacted their realtors as soon as they saw us arrive with our truck full of guns and marijuana plants—and let's not forget our pet raccoon. We were quite a sight! Needless to say, there was no Christian heritage or legacy in my family. Directly across the street from our new home, though, was a family who fascinated me.

The Tuckers were everything that the Seamans were not. They were stable, loving, supportive, and compassionate, and they were always going to church. I remember sneaking over one Christmas morning, as another fight was going on at my house, and looking in their window. I saw them all gathered around their father as he read the story of Christ's birth. I longed to have what they had. Fortunately, the Tuckers were not the type of people to keep what they had to themselves. They really would have had every reason to tell their kids not to associate with this foul-mouthed, scraggly, broken kid. But that isn't what they did. They opened their doors to me. Like, literally, they left their house unlocked through the garage door every night so that I could escape to their house if the pain at mine was too great. Mrs. Tucker said she never knew if I was going to come down the stairs in the morning with her son Mark for breakfast, and when I close my eyes I can still taste her silver dollar pancakes.

I received Christ as my Savior in their living room when I was sixteen. A few years later I felt the Lord calling me into ministry. With my background, I figured I was hearing wrong. Mark Tucker was going into ministry. He came from the right family—I didn't. One day Mark asked if I would sit in on one of his Bible college classes with him. I agreed. The professor stopped his lecture, declared that he had to obey God, looked right at me, and began to chastise "somebody" in the room for running from a call into ministry. After dismissing the class for a break, he asked me when I was going to enroll in Bible college. I enrolled that day.

I (Diana) am the granddaughter of a minister. My nana is the godliest woman I have ever known. Every year at Christmas she would put up her "Jesus stocking" and ask people to put money in the stocking that they would have spent on gifts for her. She would then take that money and buy food and gifts for the poor in her community.

I had the most stable upbringing imaginable. My dad worked hard for the Southern Pacific Railroad. My mom was a homemaker. They loved each other faithfully until my mom died of cancer in 2015 after being nursed though it by my dad. We lived in the same home my entire childhood. The main source of pain I had growing up was that *The Wonderful World of Disney* was only on TV on Sunday nights and we were always at church on Sunday night, so I only got to watch that program if someone in my family was sick.

If the church doors were open, we were there. Sunday school, Sunday morning service, Sunday evening service, Wednesday night service, vacation Bible school, and Christian summer camps were all faithfully attended and served at. My parents gave generously of themselves. They took in foster children and anyone else who needed a warm bed and some home-cooked food. Honestly, I wouldn't change my childhood for anything. I grew up with a family who loved the Lord, loved people, and loved the church. My childhood is full of rich memories.

From the age of five I knew I had a call into ministry, so after a very short foray into the world to see if it had anything to offer that was better than Jesus (spoiler alert: it didn't), off to Bible college I went. Jeff and I attended the same church and college together. It was just a matter of time before we fell in love and walked down the aisle.

Knowing that we had challenges due to our very different backgrounds and the fact that we were young (20 and 24), we sought out marriage help in the form of books read on our front porch together. We knew we didn't know all that we needed, so we went to the experts. One of the first books we read was *The Blessing* by John Trent and Gary Smalley. We decided then and there that we would be a couple who blessed each other, and someday, when God gave us children, we would be parents who passed on blessings to them.

We didn't have long to wait because our first child was born three weeks before our first anniversary. Two more precious ones followed in the next few years and we were a happy family of five, loving Jesus and serving in full-time ministry. We joke with our son, Jordan, that he was born late on a Sunday night, and that's the only reason he didn't make it to church that day. Don't worry, he was in church the following Sunday. Our other two weren't born on a Sunday, but we stopped by the church office on the way home from the hospital so that we could show them off.

Just as we did with marriage books, we began reading parenting books together because we knew we didn't know all that we needed to know. More than anything else, we wanted to get this parenting thing right. But we didn't just read books. We prayed, because in our minds, instilling a love for Jesus in our children was the most right thing we could do.

We asked the Holy Spirit to lead us as we raised these little ones. We followed God's leading in decisions regarding their upbringing. We didn't want to give them religion—we wanted them to "taste and see that the Lord is good." We wanted to be the fragrance of Christ to them. We wanted them to experience a smidgen of the vastness of their heavenly Father's love in the way that we loved them. We worked hard to give them a solid foundation in Christ, while also letting them grow and spread their wings.

Our kids all responded enthusiastically to their relationship with the Lord. They were worshipers. They served with gusto. They were all pursuing some type of call to ministry. They spoke about their faith freely. They studied Scripture faithfully. As they entered into adulthood, we could pat ourselves on the back because we had done it right. We had succeeded in making little disciples.

Goodness, we sound amazing! Maybe we should just stop writing now and let you bask in our awesomeness. Book is over. They lived happily ever after, loving and serving Jesus. The end. Let's just leave it here, our parenting successes wrapped up with a nice little bow. But that wouldn't be honest. Don't get us wrong, those things were all true about us, but obviously, if we're writing a book about prodigals, all is not puppies and rainbows in our world. We also want to be very clear that, yes, we raised our kids with love and intention, but we are human and we messed up too. Every one of our kids loves us and we have a great relationship with them, but they would have no problem telling you that we are not perfect. There have been long talks and hard conversations working through things, and heaven help us, there will probably be more.

In 2016 we had just been asked to take over a ministry opportunity that we were very excited about. The biggest thing on our minds at the time was seeking God's will for our future ministry, when one of our kids asked to stop by for a talk. That wasn't unusual, so we didn't think anything of it.

"I've decided that I no longer want to be a Christian." We had no idea those words would pierce us on a totally normal day in April. This precious child of ours, who had been raised in a pastor's home, always wanted to be in ministry, served on multiple mission trips and in countless ministries at church, dedicated an entire summer to mission work with YWAM, prayed healing over the sick, and was currently attending a Christian university, had decided to no longer claim the faith that had been professed for years. To say we were devastated would be an understatement.

Neither of us struggles with depression, but a gloom, despair, and sorrow settled on us after that day. Sometimes tears were uncontrollable and joy seemed out of reach. We were completely blindsided by something we had never thought was possible in our family. We did it right, and if you did it right, this didn't happen. We were knocked down, and it took us a while to get back up. We each handle pain differently. Jeff stress-eats (bring on the french fries and hot wings). Diana withdraws.

After we wrote this chapter and sent it off to our dear friend Chris, who is coaching us through this process, he asked us to dig a bit deeper and share more about what we went through when our child dropped this bombshell on us. Diana's first thought was, "But we told everything. We were devastated and depressed and cried a lot." Later that week we were in the car chatting about the way we handle stress. Jeff, after a painful week, had just eaten five cookies. I (Diana) said that I'm not sure how I deal with stress, but inwardly, I was thinking that I pray about it. I really couldn't say that because it sounded a little too pious, but I was sure it was true. That night, after not being able to sleep, I was reminded by the Holy Spirit exactly how I deal with pain: I cut it out. When I am hurt, I seek to remove the cause of the pain. Now, I'm a Christian and I would hesitate to admit that I ever hold any bitterness toward anybody. Instead, I frame it like this: I used to love them close, but now I just love them at arm's length. When we get hurt, my husband eats junk food, while I begin to mentally cut you out of my life. What did that look like in this situation? My first reaction that day was to take everything in the house that our child owned and shut it up in a bedroom so I couldn't see it. It hurt too much. I convinced myself that we were no longer loved or respected by our child, which was the furthest thing from the truth. The declaration that they no longer wanted to be a Christian was made shaking and in tears because of our child's great love and respect for us. I pulled back and distanced myself from my precious child and began to put up a fortress to protect myself from ever feeling that pain again. But there was a problem that actually ended up being a blessing. I loved this baby of mine too much. The protective instinct within me was trying to build up walls, but the great love within me was kicking them down. My heart was in a state of conflict. I'm happy to say that the love won, and I learned something valuable. Some people are worth hurting for.

Maybe you're feeling the same hopelessness right now. Maybe you've eaten yourself into oblivion or you're walling yourself off from pain. Let's put down the bowl of ice cream and retire the bricks and mortar. Whatever your coping mechanism is, it's time to quit coping and come into a place of honesty, healing, and hope. It's time to get up, brush yourself off, and prepare for battle. It is our hope that as we share our story with you, you will regain peace and joy. More than that, though, we want a fight to rise up within you that is powerful, steadfast, unrelenting, and victorious. We want you to have a battle cry.

At the time of this writing, our child is still not serving the Lord. We have no intention of giving you "five steps to winning your child back" or a pat formula to follow. If you would have asked us a few years ago, we probably would have given you "five steps to raising kids who always love Jesus and never say they don't want to be Christians anymore." Those book sales would have tanked by now. What we do want to give you is strength to endure, a strategy to fight for your child, and help to move you forward in the right direction.

You may have a child who wanders in the world for a month, sees enough, and comes running back home. Or you may be in for decades of navigating painful waters with a wandering child. Your circumstances will be as personal and unique as the child you're praying for.

We recently moved into the house Diana grew up in. We love this house, and as we've already told you, it's full of great memories, but it was my parents' house. It looked like them, had their flair and style. We set about remodeling everything from flooring to siding to landscaping. We used the same tools my parents had used, but the results look totally different. The hammers, paintbrushes, and shovels, in our hands, were used to create a home that was infused with our vision, style, and DNA.

As we put tools in your hands, don't expect those tools to accomplish results like ours or like someone else using the same tools. They're good tools, but you have to adapt them to your family's and child's own special makeup and circumstances.

We related our "perfect" parenting to you a little bit tongue in cheek. There actually was one parent who did do it perfectly. God the Father was the best parent two people could ever have: loving, generous, attentive. Adam and Eve were the first prodigals. They squandered what they had been given for a bite of fruit and a lie that they could have it better outside of God's will. The bottom line is that you haven't parented so wonderfully that your child would never choose to reject what you've taught and modeled before them. You also haven't blown it beyond God's redemptive power. We hope to be two very imperfect, human, mess-up-sometimes guides as we follow our perfect, divine, always-gets-it-right God together. Rest assured that both your authors and your God know your pain. We want to do everything we can to bring our child back to sweet fellowship with our Savior and then trust God to do what only He can do.

There is a glorious wedding feast coming when we get to celebrate our salvation with our Bridegroom! It is our fervent prayer that everyone who picks up this book will be at that feast, surrounded by every child they have wrestled in prayer over. Let's get to work.

A PRAYER YOU CAN PRAY

Thank you, Father, that you are a God who can relate to all we are going through. Please teach us as we read this book how to pray for and minister to our loved ones who have walked away from you. Open our ears to hear your voice, Holy Spirit, for specific strategies to use the tools you have given us, for your glory and the building of your kingdom.

CHAPTER 2

PAIN, SHAME, AND ISOLATION

Sometimes we miss being perfect parents. Ah, to be able to walk into a room, knowing that if anyone asked about our kids we could give long lists of all they were doing for the kingdom of God. If anyone's child wasn't doing well we could console them, while also smugly believing that if they had just parented right, their children would be shiny and polished like ours.

We're not perfect anymore, and to be honest, sometimes it's embarrassing. Embarrassment leads to shame and shame leads to isolation, which is exactly where the enemy wants you. If we're going to win battles against him, we can't hide out by ourselves. Our Father never intended us to face struggles alone. Because struggles are embarrassing, all too often that's exactly how we face them. We want to help you step out into the light, warts and all, so the people of God can surround you.

Having a child reject what is so important to you, what you have taught them and modeled before them, brings a myriad of wounds. The first one we want to talk about is unfulfilled expectations.

In their wonderful book *The Blessing*, Gary Smalley and John Trent outline five different blessings that modern parents pass down (or in some cases fail to pass down) to their children. These blessings correlate to the blessings we see the patriarchs give their children in Scripture. They are: meaningful touch, spoken word, attaching high value, active commitment, and picturing a special future.

Most of us, because we love and value our children, picture a special future for them. This can go too far, as we have seen parents attempt to live out their own unfulfilled dreams in their children. But in its healthy form, it is a beautiful thing to imagine the wonderful person your child will be and the things they will accomplish, especially for the Lord. Those imaginings can turn painful and come back to haunt us when they don't come to fruition.

Our child was engaged to someone in ministry when we were told of their decision to walk away from Christ. The wedding was two months away. We, and their future spouse, were convinced it was a temporary decision brought on by the stress of a wedding and graduation from university. As we got closer to the wedding, to our relief that seemed to be the case. Our child even affirmed that they were working through their questions of faith and doing much better.

The wedding went forward with everything we had dreamed of. We prayed over our child before the wedding and with the new in-laws during the ceremony. The new couple took communion and prayed together after they were pronounced "man and wife." It was a beautiful day. We had made it through a major trial, but now we believed our child was serving the Lord again and would settle into ministry alongside a godly spouse.

The reality was quite different. The struggling with faith continued. The struggle in the marriage seemed to be even worse. Four years later those precious ones were divorced. Our beloved child, though not antagonistic toward Christianity, does not profess to be a follower of Christ. We feel the need to pause here and make it clear that the divorce was not only our child's fault. We have been able to have some great talks with our child as they work through what went wrong in that marriage.

We are proud of many of the ways our child handled situations and the growth we have seen in them.

However, the special future we pictured: a godly marriage, serving in ministry, and (most importantly) a passionate love for Jesus, crumbled before our eyes. The pain was extreme.

As the shock set in, we had to come to grips with our worst fears being realized. From conception we have prayed for all of our children, that they would have a deep desire and love for the Lord, that they would follow and serve Him all the days of their lives, and that they would be used in His hands. Our kids grew up with us praying together with them over hurts, dreams, and life decisions.

We had seen some of our friends' kids walk away from the Lord, but that could just never happen in our case. We were too diligent. That one of our kids would not wholeheartedly follow after Christ was unimaginable. Until it was real. Then we figured it was only temporary because we were praying so hard and so faithfully. Until the years passed and our biggest "impossible" fear came true.

Can you begin to see how this is prime territory for the enemy to launch his attacks? Once dreams have fallen apart and fears have taken hold, we can begin doubting vital truths like the effectiveness of our prayers and the promises of God. Scripture warns us that our enemy is cunning.

"Now the serpent was more crafty than any of the wild animals the Lord God had made" (Genesis 3:1).

When you are hurt and scared, Satan will not give you a breather to regain your strength. There's no water break. He will intentionally take this opportunity to hit you with more blows. Those attacks often come in five ways: from your child, from your spouse, from others, from the powers of darkness, and from the theater in your own head.

ATTACKS FROM YOUR CHILD

Whenever a child rejects what we hold dear, there is a wound, whether it's acknowledged or not. By their actions, our son or daughter has essentially said that we're wrong and they know better. Even if those words are never uttered, they are implied. We know it and they know it and it hurts.

As is often the case, however, there are words—lots of them. There may be words telling you how you've fallen short, words recalling every parenting misstep you've ever made, words attacking your character, your friends, your God. There may be misunderstandings or misinterpretations of things you have done or said. There may even be outright lies about who you are. We are going to give you tools to handle these attacks in chapter 9. For right now, though, you simply need to know that they may come.

ATTACKS FROM YOUR SPOUSE

We hope you are reading this book together as a couple, but we are aware that that is not always feasible. One of the greatest strains on a marriage is struggles with a child. Please remember that you are on the same team. If there need to be adjustments in how either of you is relating to your child, talk it over, pray about it, give grace, and come away unified.

A friend told us the story of a couple who attends his church. At a party they lost track of their toddler. She was found in the pool. As they prepared to follow the ambulance to the hospital, the husband told his wife, "We are together on this." What did he mean? He meant that a horrible accident had happened, and they were not going to make it worse by blaming and resenting each other.

It's easy to point fingers and spew angry words during painful situations. As you walk this road, you will need love, support, and encouragement from your spouse. Don't erode that by attacking each other.

ATTACKS FROM OTHERS

There is a well-known Christian author and leader we both admire. We read a blog post about this author that discredited her character and ministry because one of her daughters is divorced. The writer of the blog literally searched for the certificate of divorce, so she could see the reason, "irreconcilable differences," and declare that it was invalid. Having had a child go through a divorce, we know the pain for all involved. How cruel to simply parade someone's perceived fault on the internet without any compassion, care, or even the most basic understanding of what the family may have gone through and the tears that were undoubtedly shed over the situation.

People will judge you. You don't need to defend yourself, and you never need to defend your love and support for your child. When people, whether well meaning or ill meaning, ask us about our prodigal, we are honest. Depending on the relationship, we give them the current information with varying levels of detail, but we always highlight the ways we are proud of our child. We affirm that we are in prayer together and with others, and we ask them to pray as well. Some will make assumptions or talk about your family behind closed doors. In some cases you may even be asked to step down from leadership in a Christian organization or church.

We are going to do a more in-depth study of the parable of the prodigal in the next chapter. However, it's interesting to note that Jesus told this parable, along with the parables of the lost sheep and lost coin, after being criticized for eating with sinners. Don't ever allow the condescending comments of others to make you believe you need to distance yourself in any way from your wandering child. Jesus ate with sinners. Be like Jesus, not the Pharisees, in your interactions with your child, and don't let anybody shame you for it.

ATTACKS FROM THE ENEMY

Second Corinthians 2:11 tells us that we are not to be unaware of the enemy's schemes.

Let's expose his schemes. He will use all of the attacks we've discussed in this chapter to strip you of your identity in Christ, your witness to your family, and your ministry to others. He will reiterate any destructive words that you've heard over and over until the peace and joy that are yours in the Spirit seep right out of you. He will seek to change your posture before God so that you approach His throne with timidity and anxiety.

He needs you to feel like an utter and complete failure, so you won't dare minister to the child who has wounded you. You wouldn't think of ministering to someone else when you have made such a mess of your own family, and how could you even pray when God must be mad at you for failing to raise a godly child?

He's a thief and a liar. He uses his lies to steal away the power, strength, faith, and hope that belong to you through Jesus. Put on your seat belts for chapter 6 because we are going to fight back!

We're going to continue peeling back the layers of his tactics, so we can recognize his lies quickly. As the pain and embarrassment grow, shame settles in to make itself at home. Once we allow the lies to take root, they begin to distort who we believe we are. If not uprooted, they become part of our identity.

ATTACKS FROM YOUR OWN THOUGHTS

We must nip these thoughts in the bud and defeat them with the truth of who we are in Christ. If we don't, they will quickly grow into hopelessness, despair, and impotence.

"We demolish arguments and every pretension that sets itself up against the knowledge of God, and we take captive every thought to make it obedient to Christ" (2 Corinthians 10:5).

When our son was sixteen, he started mowing the empty field next door to us. The owner was an older lady who couldn't do it herself. Plus, since we live in California and there is always fire danger, it gave us peace of mind to know that the dry weeds were kept under control. Before too long, we noticed a change in our own beautifully manicured lawn: weeds were beginning to sprout up. The unintended consequence of our lawn mower picking up weeds in the field next door was that that same lawn mower deposited those seed in our grass. Because we did not take quick action to eradicate them, the weeds took over.

Our enemy is an accuser. It's what he does.

"Now have come the salvation and the power and the kingdom of our God, and the authority of his Messiah. For the accuser of our brothers and sisters, who accuses them before our God day and night, has been hurled down" (Revelation 12:10).

Those weeds of accusation must be identified and removed quickly, whether they come from your child, your spouse, friends, family, strangers, or your own thoughts. If you don't pluck them out, they will grow into shame and start spreading through other areas of your life. They will affect your relationship with your child, other family members and friends, and even with God.

You are still your child's parent and spiritual mentor. Shame will keep you from walking in that calling. You still need to correct, advise, encourage, and enjoy your child. Shame will tell you that you don't have the right to do any of that. The enemy uses shame to keep your child's most powerful influencer silent and impotent.

Shame convinces you to adopt a "they can't know" attitude toward others. We hate to break it to you, but they know. At minimum, they have suspicions.

We have an extended family member who is gay. Years ago, another family member tried to shush someone who mentioned it, falsely believing that none of us knew. We all knew. Even before the days of social media, most things were not that hard to figure out.

Thinking that we have something to hide makes us pull away from the ones we need to surround and support us. Perhaps the greatest damage that shame can do is in our relationship with God. If our heads are hung low, how can we come boldly before His throne?

"Let us then approach God's throne of grace with confidence, so that we may receive mercy and find grace to help us in our time of need" (Hebrews 4:16).

As we talked about in the previous chapter, we grew up in very different households. Diana grew up in church every Sunday with loving Christian parents. Jeff grew up in a broken home full of abuse, drugs, and alcohol. We both have struggles, but one of us struggles with identity more than the other. I bet you can guess who.

When I (Jeff) became a Christian at age sixteen, I had a skewed image of God as my Father. I was a wrestler in high school, and I used to be terrified to sin on Wednesdays because those were wrestling days, and if I sinned, surely God wouldn't allow me to win my matches. The exacting demands of my father caused me to view God as if He would punish and toss me aside at the slightest infraction. At first it was a relationship based more on fear of failing Him than on confidence in His love for me.

Parents who heap abuse and rejection on their child end up with a child who is not confident of their position in the family or the love of the parent. Friends, that is not who our Father is!

"The Lord is compassionate and gracious, slow to anger, abounding in love" (Psalm 103:8).

When shame causes us to view God through the wrong lens, we will find ourselves pulling away from our greatest ally in our battle against the enemy to win our child back.

That is right where Satan wants us: heads hung low in shame, pulling away from other believers because we are convinced they will reject us, and even staying away from the one who holds the power to comfort, encourage, and work the miracle of salvation in our loved ones. If we do not bring the truth of God's Word and His character to the shame that has taken root, we will grow more and more isolated.

As we continue the downward spiral, depression takes hold. There were entire days that we lost to tears and despair after conversations with our child. Thankfully, we fought back quickly and just lost some days here and there. We know of parents who have lost months and years to a depression that settles on them because of shame and isolation. We have a friend who tearfully admitted, at a prayer meeting, that she had completely stopped praying for her child. It was too painful, and she felt that God wasn't listening.

As the isolation continues, we develop a distorted view of reality. We were meant to be in relationship with other believers in true communion. That means a sharing of life in all of its joys and pains.

"Rejoice with those who rejoice; mourn with those who mourn" (Romans 12:15).

Without this true fellowship with safe people who will hold your heart, you begin to believe the airbrushed and sugarcoated version of everyone's social media lives. Everyone else seems to have happy, problem-free families, and the pain and despair just increase.

Now the thoughts begin to gravitate toward the unfairness of it all. We may not dare say it, but the goodness of God gets brought into question. How come everyone else doesn't have problems as big as ours? How come all of that family's children are serving in ministry? Have I displeased God?

PAIN, SHAME, AND ISOLATION

We have a friend who is the daughter of a pastor. She adores her parents and has struggled to understand why some pastors enjoy all their children serving the Lord while in her family, her brother struggled with drug addiction for years. He is clean and sober now but caused great pain to her godly parents.

Let's pause and take stock of the damage the enemy can wreak because one child walks away from the Lord. From that initial pain, there is the potential for shame, isolation, broken relationships, pulling away from God's presence, depression, comparison, and resentment toward the blessings of others.

"The acts of the flesh are obvious: sexual immorality, impurity and debauchery; idolatry and witchcraft; hatred, discord, jealousy, fits of rage, selfish ambition, dissensions, factions and envy; drunkenness, orgies, and the like. I warn you, as I did before, that those who live like this will not inherit the kingdom of God. But the fruit of the Spirit is love, joy, peace, forbearance, kindness, goodness, faithfulness, gentleness and self-control" (Galatians 5:19–23).

This is a breeding ground for the acts of the flesh to grow, multiply, and ultimately cause our defeat. But those beautiful fruits of the Spirit: joy, peace, love, kindness . . We do not have to wait for everything to be as perfect as our Instagram pictures to walk in those things. They are by the Spirit, which means they are unaffected by what is happening in the natural.

As we open up our hearts and lives to others and let them see the ugly things, too, the power of shame and isolation is broken. In her excellent book *Chasing Vines*, Beth Moore writes about how she can't "fix" her family no matter how hard she tries. Just reading those words is a balm to the weary parent who wonders if they are the only one who has pain in their family.

"But we have this treasure in jars of clay to show that this all-surpassing power is from God and not from us. We are hard pressed on every side, but not crushed; perplexed, but not in despair; persecuted, but not abandoned; struck down, but not destroyed" (2 Corinthians 4:7–9).

The world needs to see that Jesus is not dependent on your perfection. He loves you and can use you and bless you even if your children make you weep at times. A few years ago we decided to gather some parents of prodigals together to pray for our children. We called it Battle Cry. As we finished our first little Battle Cry prayer meeting, we all talked about the relief of authenticity and knowing that we were not alone. We were amazed that, although nothing had changed in the natural, we all felt as if a load had been lifted. We had genuine joy and peace because they were not dependent on the actions of our children or others but were birthed within us from the Holy Spirit.

CHAPTER 3

THE PRODIGAL AND THE FATHER'S HEART

A s we walk this road it is vital that we align our hearts, actions, and thoughts with our heavenly Father's regarding our child. What would God do in our situation? Fortunately, Jesus told us our own story in the parable of the prodigal. We know how the father in this story must have felt. But more importantly, the Father knows how we feel. Before we move on, we want to take a closer look at the parable of the prodigal son in Luke 15:11–24:

> Jesus continued: "There was a man who had two sons. The younger one said to his father, 'Father, give me my share of the estate.' So he divided his property between them.

> "Not long after that, the younger son got together all he had, set off for a distant country and there squandered his wealth in wild living. After he had spent everything, there was a severe famine in that whole country, and he began to be in need. So he went and hired himself out to a citizen of that country, who sent him to his fields to feed pigs. He longed to fill his stomach with

the pods that the pigs were eating, but no one gave him anything.

"When he came to his senses, he said, 'How many of my father's hired servants have food to spare, and here I am starving to death! I will set out and go back to my father and say to him: Father, I have sinned against heaven and against you. I am no longer worthy to be called your son; make me like one of your hired servants.' So he got up and went to his father.

"But while he was still a long way off, his father saw him and was filled with compassion for him; he ran to his son, threw his arms around him and kissed him.

"The son said to him, 'Father, I have sinned against heaven and against you. I am no longer worthy to be called your son.'

"But the father said to his servants, 'Quick! Bring the best robe and put it on him. Put a ring on his finger and sandals on his feet. Bring the fattened calf and kill it. Let's have a feast and celebrate. For this son of mine was dead and is alive again; he was lost and is found.' So they began to celebrate."

Many of us are so familiar with this story that we can easily miss the shocking nature of the younger son's request. Kenneth E. Bailey is a missionary to the Middle East who has written a fascinating book called *The Cross and the Prodigal: Luke 15 Through the Eyes of Middle Eastern Peasants*. Whenever he is speaking about this parable in villages, he always asks if any son in that village has ever made the same request. Every time, the villagers are shocked and indignant, insisting that none of their sons would ever ask such a thing. Why? Because the son's request meant that he wanted his father to die.

We realize that all of us are thinking about our own children while reading this story, but can we stop for just a moment and humbly admit that we have all, at times, wanted God out of the way so we can live our lives how we want? We would never say we want God to die, but we have all been guilty of wanting him to bless us and then get out of our way so we can do as we please, just like the younger son. We have all been prodigals.

Not only does the son want his father out of the way, he also wants to relinquish all responsibility for the family. The inheritance was given with the expectation of taking care of the family, the estate, the servants, and the livestock and maintaining the family reputation. The son doesn't want to do any of that. He just wants the money. Again, there is a caution for us here. When we simply want the blessings of God but refuse to give of ourselves to His kingdom, His mission, and the care of our church community, we are following in the footsteps of the younger son.

Another shocking part of this story is that the father grants his son's request. That was completely countercultural to the people Jesus was telling this parable to. As far as they were concerned, the just and correct response would have been for the father to deny this insulting, shameful request and then punish the son. We've barely gotten started, and already this story is scandalous.

The son is granted his share of the inheritance, quickly liquidates it, and then heads off to another country to live it up. Scripture tells us that he "squandered his wealth in wild living." The word prodigal means squanderer. What the younger son did was unforgivable. In that culture to squander the family wealth was bad enough. To squander the family wealth among the gentiles was traitorous.

The prodigal has now reached the point of no return. His sins are too great. He has insulted and humiliated his father and family, and worse, he has done it among the gentiles. He will never be allowed back in his village again. If he tries to come home, no one in the village will welcome him, help him, feed him, or shelter him. If he attempts to enter the village, the *kezazah* ceremony will be performed. As soon as they see him coming, the elders, surrounded by everyone else, will meet him before he sets foot in the village. They will smash a pot at his feet, communicating to him that he is not welcome there anymore. Kezazah means "to cut off." Our prodigal is on his own in a foreign land.

After he has spent everything, tragedy strikes and there is a famine in the land. Sin will always produce a famine of some sort. In your child's case it may be a famine of love, peace, joy, finances, or a myriad of other things. The prodigal begins to feel his need.

He looks for a solution to his problem. He tries to fill the void but just ends up in squalor and misery. He has reached his low point.

We hear your heart and we echo its cries. You don't want your precious child to feel hungry. You don't want your child to have to suffer a famine of the soul, body, mind, or emotions. It's agonizing to imagine what it could take to bring your child to his or her senses. The Father knows how you feel.

The prodigal in Jesus's story finally comes to his senses and remembers the goodness of his father and his father's house. But there's a problem. He knows he cannot go home. He has squandered the family's money among the gentiles. Maybe, if he can pay back the money, he can earn his way back into the community. So he hatches a plan.

Armed with the appearance of humility, he uses words similar to those of Pharaoh in Exodus 10:16 to get his father to help him one more time. He will ask his father to make him like one of the hired servants. He is not asking to be a slave—he wants to be a **hired** servant. He is asking for a job, most likely an apprenticeship. If he can get his father to help him secure an apprenticeship, he can pay the money back and remove the shame and separation that his sin has caused. He believes he can work his way back into the good graces of his family and his community. Up to this point, he thinks his sin against his father is all about the money. He couldn't be more wrong.

We don't know exactly what the father has been doing this whole time. We do know that he allowed his son to make destructive choices, choices that were harmful to both the son and the family. Free will is truly a gift from God. We once heard someone compare God to an abusive boyfriend who has to control the ones he loves. This parable shatters that notion, and the destructive chaos in our world proves it to be false. God in His great mercy gives us all we need to live fruitful and righteous lives. We have salvation through Jesus, we have the Holy Spirit to empower and guide us, and we have Scripture to instruct us. Yet like the prodigal, we want all the blessings and then ask God to step aside and let us live our own lives. The unbelievable thing is that He does. After we squander our blessings, destroy relationships, and mess everything up, we have two choices: we can rage at God because He doesn't control everyone's actions and force us into a utopia, or we can give up and humbly return to Him. What will we find if we choose the latter?

Verse 20 tells us that while the son was still a long way off, the father was filled with compassion and ran to meet him. This story that Jesus is telling just keeps getting crazier and crazier! The father ran? That's unheard of. According to Kenneth E. Bailey, Middle Eastern men **never** run—they walk in a dignified manner. To run, the father would have had to gather up his robe, tuck it into his belt, and show his bare legs, like a boy. That was shameful and humiliating. But there the father goes, running with all his might for the whole village to see, humiliating himself in front of all of them to get to that son whom he loves.

Right after our child's divorce, we felt the pang of shame every time someone would ask how the happy couple was doing and we had to divulge the truth. How hypocritical! How many of our own actions should have left us shamed by God, yet He runs.

The father has to run because it's important for him to get there quickly. Remember the kezazah ceremony? He must beat everyone else to his son. He cannot allow the son he loves to be cut off and declared unwelcome.

Something happens now in the son's heart. He had such a well-thought-out plan and a rehearsed speech. That falls by the wayside when he sees his father's total willingness to open himself up to ridicule for the sake of his child. The son realizes something. His greatest sin was never the money. It wasn't the wild living or the squandering. His greatest sin was breaking his father's heart and walking away from that relationship. After all the pleasures and all the hardships, it is seeing the great love and sacrifice of his father that finally breaks him. He cannot earn his way back. He cannot make enough money to repay the pain he has caused the one who runs to him now. He cannot work his way back into the family. In true repentance he gives up his plan, and all he can utter is that he has sinned and is not worthy to be a son.

This father running and enduring humiliation to rescue his undeserving child is a beautiful picture of the cross. Hebrews 12:2 tells us that "for the joy set before him" Jesus endured the cross. Luke 9:51 says that Jesus "resolutely set out for Jerusalem," where He would be crucified. Our Savior ran with determination, compassion, and His eyes on the prize (us!) to the humiliation and brutality of the cross. "But God demonstrates his own love for us in this: While we were still sinners, Christ died for us" (Romans 5:8). Kenneth E. Bailey says, "This parable depicts a father who leaves the comfort and security of his home and humiliates himself before the village. The coming down and going out to his son is a parable of the incarnation." As we know, our God doesn't only save, He restores. The father has saved his son from being cut off, but now he goes even further.

The father in our story doesn't have to work up love for his son. The love has been there every single day watching for a sign of the son's return. The loving relationship with his father has been available to the son at any moment—he simply needed to allow his father's embrace and kiss. The welcome that the father gives the son immediately lets the villagers know how the father expects his son to be treated. Furthermore, the father orders the servants to dress his son. The father is establishing the fact that his child will be restored to sonship, not become a hired hand.

The father has his son dressed in his best robe. This probably would have been a robe that the father himself had worn (see Esther 6:1–9). Again, the imagery is beautiful. "For all of you who were baptized into Christ have clothed yourselves with Christ" (Galatians 3:27).

The ring placed on the son's finger signifies his authority in the family. He can once again make legal decisions and sign documents. This will be an important thing to remember when we discuss spiritual warfare in chapter 6.

The servants are told to put sandals on his feet. Servants were often barefoot. The father is restoring his son into the full rights of sonship.

Now the fattened calf is brought in for a celebration. This would have been no ordinary party, and the whole village would have been invited. The father is not ashamed of his son. He is celebrating loudly and publicly that his child has returned home.

If we're honest, the father's actions can seem a bit too merciful for our liking. They were certainly too merciful for the older son's liking. Does the father seem weak to you? Maybe he's just setting himself up to be taken advantage of again.

Let's look at what the father doesn't do. He doesn't give his son the cold shoulder. He doesn't care about his own reputation. He doesn't tell the son about how many tears he has shed or how many hours he has spent looking for the son's return. He never brings up the money. He doesn't point out how many cutbacks he had to make around the farm because of the son's greed. He doesn't heap guilt or abuse on his son. He doesn't even agree to make him a hired servant, which would have been extremely merciful.

The father goes so lavishly beyond what is reasonable, fair, and deserved to completely and totally save his son and restore him to all the rights of sonship. This is the same God who proclaimed in Joel 2:25 (ESV), "I will restore to you the years that the swarming locust has eaten." His readmittance into the family has come with no strings attached.

Jesus has done exactly the same thing to every one of us who has fallen on our knees before Him knowing that we are not worthy. He has saved and restored us so completely. We should tremble in fear if we refuse to treat our own children the way God, through Jesus, has treated us "For if you forgive other people when they sin against you, your heavenly Father will also forgive you" (Matthew 6:14).

We understand that sometimes boundaries must be set for children who are not walking in genuine repentance. However, our hearts need to always be ready to forgive any and every wound that child has caused us and run to embrace them at the first sign of repentance, not wait until they have proven themselves to be perfect.

A few years ago we received the joy of our very first grandchild. Our son and daughter-in-law were both in their early twenties when he was born. During the months leading up to his birth, we were asked quite often if they were ready for a baby. Since it came up so frequently, we really thought about whether they were ready. Our son had never changed a diaper. They didn't make much money. They lived in a one-bedroom apartment. They hadn't had much time together as a married couple before she got pregnant. Our answer became, "They are 100 percent ready to love that child with everything they have, so yes, they are ready."

Our words were true. They were ready with all they needed. Sebastian is healthy and happy in every way. Wesley and Tori delight in that precious boy. Wesley has definitely changed his fair share of diapers by now, but that was never a prerequisite. A determination to love their child through any and everything was the only real requirement.

Yes, our children will hurt us. The pain the younger son inflicted on the father was extreme. The pain we inflict on our heavenly Father is extreme. But there is something so powerful about genuine love and mercy. This needs to be a prayer of ours daily:

Father, equip us to love lavishly, to pour buckets of grace and mercy on our child. Help us to remember that we have been forgiven much. Make our hearts strong to endure whatever pain or humiliation running to our prodigal may bring. May our love for our child point them to your even greater love.

CHAPTER 4

REGAIN YOUR FOOTING

When I (Diana) was sixteen years old, I got my first speeding ticket. I cried and cried, but the officer was unmoved. My cousin and I were on our way to a concert, and it ruined the whole evening for me. I knew I would have to tell my dad and appear before a judge. Both prospects made my stomach churn. I knew I should tell my dad face-to-face, but I chickened out and called him from my cousin's house after the concert. He told me to come straight home, and I was filled with anxiety during the drive.

Before you think that my dad is scary, you should know that he is the opposite. He is amazing, kind, loving, generous, and supportive. That's what bothered me the most. I was afraid he would be disappointed in me. He also had the power to take my car away, and I have to admit, that added to my fear as well.

When I arrived home, I went sheepishly into the house. My dad simply said, "I never killed your brother, so I won't kill you." Then he smiled and went to bed. My dad also has a sense of humor. It felt like a weight was lifted off my shoulders. My dad and I were still OK.

A few weeks later I had to appear before a judge. I was scared again. The judge was in no way mean to me, but he had a job to do, and he could only be as merciful as the law allowed. He enforced the fine I had to pay and sent me to traffic school, so I could learn to do better next time.

Although I had more at stake in the relationship with my dad, given the choice, I would much rather be judged by my father. Because of his great love for me, there were no limits to the mercy he was willing to give me.

Please don't ever forget that because you are a follower of Jesus, God now relates to you as a Father, not a judge.

Now that we've seen what it looks like to be a child of the Father, let's stop and really take a look at ourselves as children of the King. Has the shame, worry, or embarrassment of having a child walk away from God caused you to hang your head low, feel unworthy, or get stuck in cycles of regret and blame? In chapter 6 we will discuss spiritual warfare. However, if you are going to go to war, you must be confidently ready for battle, and that means tearing down anything that may be robbing you of your true identity in Christ.

Innumerable books have been written on identity and specifically our identity in Christ. Yet it is something that Christians still struggle with. The way you view yourself is important to God. So much so that He changed some of His followers' names in the past, so they would see themselves in a new light. In this chapter we are going to take a look at some people in Scripture who had their names changed and then talk about how that relates to us, how God views us, and how we have to start viewing ourselves.

This is not simply some self-help encouragement or a motivational speech. It is vital—we'll even go so far as to say a matter of life and death—that you understand your identity in Christ and all of the blessings, power, and authority that come along with that. God expects you to believe them and walk in them.

In Genesis 12 we are introduced to a man named Abram (meaning "high father") who is married to Sarai (meaning "princess"). God speaks to Abram, giving him a promise and a command. God promises to make

Abram into a great nation and bless him. God then commands Abram to leave his father's house and go to another land.

We don't know much about Abram at this point. Later in this chapter we see that he has a propensity toward fear, deception, and self-preservation. However, one of the greatest characteristics of Abram is that when God speaks, he immediately obeys.

In Genesis 17, twenty-four years after God made His promise to Abram, God comes again and reminds Abram of the promise. Abram is a little skeptical now because he is ninety-nine years old and still doesn't have a child with his wife, Sarai. Abram has tried to do things his way and had a son with Hagar, Sarai's servant, but that was never God's plan.

Now God gives the command of circumcision. There needs to be a cutting away of the flesh. The human way of doing things is not going to cut it (pun intended). It is now that God changes the names of Abram and Sarai to Abraham ("father of a multitude") and Sarah ("mother of nations").

They are new! They are different! They are not to do things their own way, in their own power anymore. They have a new identity that has its foundation in the promises of God and His power alone. They don't have to muster up this identity. It is given to them because of God's promise and their simple obedience.

Years later Abraham and Sarah indeed have a growing family. Their son, Isaac, has twin sons named Esau ("hairy") and Jacob ("supplanter" or "deceiver"). Jacob is born after Esau but literally comes out of the womb grabbing Esau's heel. Although it was only by mere seconds, Esau, as the older brother, would have been the heir, with all the benefits, perks, and responsibility for the family. He would have also received a great blessing from his father.

The problem was that Jacob was a trickster. He lived up to his name. First he got Esau to trade his birthright for a bowl of stew. Then he tricked his father into giving him Esau's blessing. After that, Jacob runs for his life from Esau. You can read all about the boys' stories in Genesis 25–33.

But God had a soft spot for Jacob. Even when the boys were still in the womb, God had said that the older would serve the younger (Genesis 25:23). Jacob and Esau don't meet up again for many years. By this time Jacob has a large family and is quite wealthy. As you can imagine, he's a bit nervous to meet his older (and larger) brother. Jacob takes every precaution he can think of to protect his family from Esau. After sending them ahead, he is left alone.

God shows up and has a wrestling match with Jacob. Jacob refuses to let God go until He blesses him. Jacob gets his blessing—along with a dislocated hip. What was the blessing? A new name, Israel. No longer is he Jacob the deceiver. He is now Israel ("having power with God"). That's quite a difference!

Jacob/Israel and his entire family end up living in Egypt. Things are good at first, but after a few hundred years, the Egyptians make the Israelites their slaves. The Israelites cry out to the God of Abraham, Isaac, and Jacob/Israel for a deliverer from their bondage. You know the story. God sends them Moses, who leads them out of slavery and gives them the law. But their sin problem remains a big issue. They still have not been truly set free, and they long for a messiah.

Fast-forward thousands of years. God is now a man, Jesus, living on the planet He created among the people He loves. He meets a fisherman named Simon ("God has heard"). In John 1:42, right after Jesus and Simon meet, Jesus changes Simon's name to Peter ("rock").

Later, in Matthew 16:18–19, Jesus expounds on Peter's name a bit more. "I tell you that you are Peter, and on this rock I will build my church, and the gates of Hades [or realm of the dead] will not overcome it. I will give you the keys of the kingdom of heaven; whatever you bind on earth will be bound in heaven, and whatever you loose on earth will be loosed in heaven." That's quite a destiny for a common fisherman!

God is in the business of taking small, bumbling, unsure, mistake-making, weak, failing, insecure people and changing them into people of power, strength, destiny, blessing, authority, and confidence.

"But God chose the foolish things of the world to shame the wise; God chose the weak things of the world to shame the strong. God chose the lowly things of this world and the despised things—and the things that are not—to nullify the things that are, so that no one may boast before him" (1 Corinthians 1:27–29).

Abram, Jacob, and Simon were not great men. They were ordinary, and they messed things up. They got scared and confused. Yet God transformed them into men of extraordinary destiny, and He marked that change by changing their names.

What name do you attach to yourself? Failure? Insignificant? Weak? Stupid?

For years our identity was wrapped up in having a family of ministry-working lovers of Jesus. Missions trips, check! Christian camp counselors, check! Leaders in the youth group, check! Following a call into ministry, attending Christian university, helping in Children's Church, check, check, check! Our kids did it all, and we were so proud—you might even say boastful.

When we had a child tell us they were no longer a Christian, the things that had built up our identity (along with the value that came with it) crashed down like the house of cards it was. We went from finding our value in being model parents who had cracked the code of perfect Christian parenting to believing that we were complete failures who must have made some unforgivable parenting mistake.

The reality is that neither of those things was ever true. Just like Abram, Jacob, and Simon, we're not perfect. We have certainly made parenting mistakes. We've also had some great parenting successes. We've gotten it right sometimes and wrong sometimes.

But also like Abram, Jacob, and Simon, God didn't turn His back on us because of the mistakes, and He is certainly not impressed with the successes. It is God who declares who we are, and it is not based on our works but on His faithfulness.

What name does God attach to you? Royalty! Chosen! Loved! Powerful! Authoritative! Wise! And finally, parent! The moment your first child was born or adopted, God changed your name to parent. That's a big deal, and there is destiny attached to that name.

When the enemy seduced and lied to your child to lead them away from God's love and purpose for them, he started a war. You need to be ready to bust through the gates of hell and make him sorry that he messed with your child.

Remember when Jesus expounded on Peter's name and declared that the gates of hell cannot stand against the attack of the church? Peter must have felt ten feet tall when Jesus said that. But five verses later, Jesus is saying to Peter, "Get behind me, Satan! You are a stumbling block to me; you do not have in mind the concerns of God, but merely human concerns."

What happened to Peter, the rock on which the church would be built? He allowed his words to come into alignment with the will of Satan instead of the wisdom of God. He tried to get Jesus to act in a way that made sense to Peter instead of fulfilling the will of the Father.

What is the will of Satan for you? Jesus tells us in John 10:10 that he comes to steal from you and your children, kill you and your children, and destroy you and your children. It's up to you to stop him, and he will attempt anything and everything to make you think you can't. He will tell you that you're weak, foolish, dumb, uneducated, and a hypocrite. He will remind you of every time you've gotten it wrong in the hope that you will be too demoralized to even think about entering into battle. He's terrified because he knows how much of a threat you are to him and his work. Before you run into battle, you must shake off the labels he is trying to put on you and come into alignment with who God says you are!

How do we do that?

REPENT OF SIN

We like to say, "Keep short accounts with God." If you've sinned, take it to God immediately. Humbly repent and ask Him for ways to avoid temptation in the future.

REPENT OF BELIEVING THE LABELS THE ENEMY PLACES ON YOU

Remember Revelation 12:10? He is the accuser of the saints. Jesus is your defender. When you wallow in your failures, you are taking sides with and believing your accuser over your defender. Stop it! The only one who has earned your allegiance is the one who hung on a cross, experienced death, and rose from the grave so that you could walk in complete righteousness.

ASK THE HOLY SPIRIT TO REVEAL THE ENEMY'S SCHEMES

"Then the dragon was enraged at the woman and went off to wage war against the rest of her offspring—those who keep God's commands and hold fast their testimony about Jesus" (Revelation 12:17).

You are being stalked and hunted by a predator. He watches for weaknesses. He pounces in moments of vulnerability. Do you notice that your identity plummets when you're tired? Or maybe, after you've interacted with a certain person, you feel worthless? Do some holidays make you feel like a failure? The enemy will have schemes against you and will attempt to hit you when you're already down. Ask the Holy Spirit to illuminate these instances. Make sure you prepare for them in prayer. Recruit others to pray for you when you know you have a possible moment of weakness coming up.

RECOGNIZE WRONG THOUGHTS AND IMMEDIATELY TAKE THEM CAPTIVE

Returning to 2 Corinthians 10:5, don't just think your thoughts, make them pass the litmus test of God's Word. If they don't pass, they don't get to stay, period. Wallowing in lies will just take you down a spiral into pain, depression, regret, and impotence. In a few chapters, we're going to talk about how to ask for forgiveness from those you may have wronged (including your child). We're pretty positive that, if you're reading this book, you have messed up before. One of the most powerful things about Satan's accusations is that some of them are true and we know it. But dear ones, the miracle of salvation is that we don't deserve it! We have failed. And yet, there is our glorious Savior willing to let His own righteousness be ours. Woo-hoo! That's what your thoughts need to be dwelling on.

RECEIVE THE BLESSING OF BEING A CHILD OF GOD

Don't just get rid of the wrong thoughts, think the right ones. Recognize the love, blessings, power, and authority that are yours because of the new name God has given you: Christian ("little Christ"). Dwell on all that is yours in Christ Jesus, and then let your gratitude pour out in worship to our generous Father.

MAKE WORSHIP A DAILY RESPITE FROM THE WEIGHT OF THE WORLD

Worship is powerful. As we lift our eyes up to bask in the beauty of our God who is mighty and majestic but also loving and kind, we are encouraged. We aren't talking about the kind of encouragement you get when someone tells you they like your outfit or new hairstyle. We are talking about being infused with courage. When we focus on God's incredible strength and His unfailing love for us, we realize that we do not need to fear anything.

READ AND MEMORIZE GOD'S WORD

How do you know who you are unless you let God's words speak loudly and often to you? Of course, we know from Matthew 4 that even Jesus used God's written Word to defeat Satan during Satan's feeble attempt to tempt Jesus away from His God-given destiny. Let God's written Word tell you who you are, and memorize it so you can remind the enemy of it when he attempts to tempt you away from your God-given destiny. Some good Scriptures to memorize are:

You are loved—John 15:9

You are forgiven—Ephesians 1:7

You are chosen—Ephesians 1:11

You are redeemed—Galatians 3:13–14

You are valued—Matthew 10:31

You are blessed—Ephesians 1:3

You are a child of God—1 John 3:1

You are a new creation—2 Corinthians 5:17

You are complete in Christ—Colossians 2:10

Let's end this chapter by taking one more look at Simon/Peter. In Matthew 26 we see Peter fail again, and this time it was really bad. Jesus had warned him, but Peter defiantly declared twice that he would never abandon Jesus. Jesus asked him to pray so he wouldn't fall into temptation, but instead of praying, Peter fell asleep. When the moment came for Peter to walk his talk, he failed and disowned Jesus. Matthew 26:75 tells us, "Then Peter remembered the word Jesus had spoken: 'Before the rooster crows, you will disown me three times.' And he went outside and wept bitterly."

We live in a rural area near Sacramento. We have roosters around here. They crow. A lot. Can you imagine what Peter must have felt every time he heard a rooster crow after that? Every morning he got woken up with the reminder of his failure.

In John's account of the story, he points out that Peter was warming himself over a fire when he denied Jesus (John 18:18). The Greek word for fire here specifies that it was a charcoal fire. We see that word again in John 21:9. Let's set the scene. Jesus has risen from the dead. Peter has gone fishing. Peter isn't fishing for men as Jesus said he would; he is fishing for fish, just like he used to. Can you blame him? He was supposed to be Peter, the rock that Jesus was going to build his church on, but that was before his epic failures. Now he's just Simon the fisherman again because he's probably sure he doesn't deserve to be anything else. He messed up all of God's plans for him. That is, until Jesus calls him to come to a charcoal fire.

There, over similar charcoal as when he denied his Savior, Jesus restores him the same number of times as his denials. That's what Jesus does. Jesus speaks words of destiny over his discouraged disciple: "feed my lambs," "take care of my sheep," "feed my sheep," and "follow me." Peter had a job to do, and that job wasn't taken away because he had some mess-ups along the way.

Doesn't Scripture tell us over and over that humility is foundational to being used by God? Maybe for Peter to be that rock the church would be built upon, he didn't need to have game, talk big, or muster up courage and zeal. Maybe the first thing we all need is to know that Jesus has purchased our rooster crows with His own blood. Peter needed to start at the same place we all do—the realization that we are not big shots. We all have places of failure and pain that we wish we could erase. We think God needs us to be great so He can use us, when in reality, God needs us to see how great He is so He can use us.

The only two mentions in the New Testament of a fire specifically being charcoal are at Peter's failure and his restoration. We believe that is intentional. Jesus didn't need to lecture Peter or go over where and why he tripped up. Jesus simply called him back to his place of failure and asked him the most important question: "Do you love me more than anything else?" If the answer to that question is yes, then Jesus has plans for you. That's your only prerequisite.

In Acts we see Peter become that courageous and zealous man that he wanted to be. However, we would argue that standing up and preaching to thousands in power and authority wasn't what made Peter that church-building rock. Peter truly became the rock of the church when he was desperate in his own striving and had nothing left but his love for Jesus. Everything he thought he was had been shattered to dust. In her book *It's Not Supposed to Be This Way*, Lisa TerKeurst points out that dust happens to be God's favorite building material. He created His favorite and most loved creation (mankind) from dust. Dust doesn't deter God. On the contrary, sometimes He needs us to finally get down to nothing but dust, so He can build us into something with purpose. This isn't only true for us, but it is true for our children as well. God simply isn't afraid of the shattered remains we, or they, have made of our lives.

Isaiah 61:3 (NLT) tells us that our God can "give a crown of beauty for ashes, a joyous blessing instead of mourning, festive praise instead of despair." What an amazing God we serve! Who else says, "Bring me your ugly pile of ashes, and I will trade you for a crown of beauty"? God Himself takes all the losses, and we get all the blessings. Yeah, we'll trade our ashes for a crown any day!

How about you? Do you need to take some time to sit with Jesus over a charcoal fire right now? Are there areas in your life that have been reduced to ashes and dust because of your own failures? Have you given up your God-given destiny because you think you've messed things up too much? Spend some time in prayer right now letting Jesus restore the beauty, plans, and purposes He has for you.

A PRAYER YOU CAN PRAY

Heavenly Father, I cannot even fathom how large your love is that you would willingly take my failures and in return give me beauty, freedom, purpose, strength, and destiny. What a great God you are. So I'll take you up on your offer. I bring you my ashes, my dust, my rooster crows. I bring you the time I _____ *. Please forgive me for times I have messed up and times I have come into alignment with the lies of the enemy instead of the truth of who you say I am. Right now I reaffirm my love for you is greater than anything else. Please give me the strength, courage, and discernment to walk in all the plans and purposes you have for me. Thank you that I am a dearly loved child of the King of Kings.*

CHAPTER 5

LET'S PRAY

We sat next to a lady at an event once who told us about her son who had walked away from his faith in the Lord. After telling us his story, she said, "I should probably start praying for him." We were shocked. She hadn't already been praying for him? At the time, we were still perfect parents and knew we would never have to go through that with any of our children. But if something crazy happened and we ever had a child reject Christ, prayer would be the first thing we would do. Well, we obviously didn't know what our future would hold. But we were correct about what our response would be—it would be prayer, immediately and often.

We have to admit that we have dragged our feet on getting this chapter written. Not because we don't love prayer. We love it, do it, and rely on it. However, at the time of this writing, the prayer we have been praying the most fervently for the past seven years has not been answered the way we would like. We have been encouraged. We have received words from the Lord. We have been led by the Holy Spirit. We are so grateful for those things, but what we really want is a tried-and-true formula and a beautiful ending tied up with a bow to share with you. How we would love to give you our "keys to praying your child back into the fold" and then top it off with our victory story. Wouldn't that be lovely?

That's not what this chapter will be. Don't worry, there will be loveliness here, but the loveliness, beauty, and greatness won't be our tidy story. It will all revolve around our magnificent God. He is faithful! He is slow to anger and abounding in love! He is powerful and mighty to save! He is compassionate! He is wise and so much more! It is vital that we begin there. When we go to God in prayer, we must start with declarations of who He is. That's called praise. We don't do it because He needs it. We do it because He is worthy of it and we need it.

You will have days when you mess up. You will have days when you do everything right but everything still goes wrong. You will have days of despair and days of victory. If your confidence and hope rest on how your day is going or how you're feeling, instability will be your constant companion. Our hope rests in one place, and that is in the unchanging character of our God. As we call out those attributes daily and praise Him, we have hope no matter our circumstances, because our hope is tethered to the right thing. That's called faith.

In his famous "Hall of Faith" chapter, the writer of Hebrews points out, "Now faith is confidence in what we hope for and assurance about what we do not see. . . . And without faith it is impossible to please God, because anyone who comes to him must believe that he exists and that he rewards those who earnestly seek him" (Hebrews 11:1, 6).

In Malachi 3:13–18, God accuses His people of speaking arrogantly against Him. They are a bit indignant and want to know how they've done such a thing. God responds by telling them that they have smeared His character by saying that it's futile to serve God because bad things still happen and evildoers still get away with stuff. The modern version of this would be "If God is so loving and powerful, why do bad things still happen?" But verse 16 says, "Those who feared the Lord talked with each other, and the Lord listened and heard. A scroll of remembrance was written in his presence concerning those who feared the Lord and honored his name." God takes what we say about Him seriously. This chapter closes with God declaring, "On the day when I act . . . they will be my treasured possession. I will spare them, just as a father has compassion and spares his son who serves him. And you will again see the distinction between the righteous and the wicked, between those who serve God and those who do not" (vv. 17–18). The difference between the wicked and the righteous is what they believe and say about God.

Sometimes the urgency to pray may not be there because whether we admit it to ourselves or not, we assume that God will do what He wants anyway and it makes no difference what we ask for. Genesis 18:16–32, Exodus 4, and Matthew 15:21–28 give us examples of people having conversations with God. God is a good conversationalist. He does not just talk and mandate what He wants, He listens and cares about what is on your heart too. In a way, prayer is a mystery. God, who is all-knowing and all-powerful, really does want us to engage with Him to present our requests. Why? We really don't know except that God is love and He loves us.

In the love chapter (1 Corinthians 13), it says that love does not "demand its own way." If God is love, then that means that God does not demand His own way. This may sound odd because many people believe that God's Word is nothing but God dictating how we will act. We would make the assertion that God's Word actually shows us the opposite. The first thing God did after creating Adam and Eve was give them a choice. Free will is the ultimate expression of love because love does not demand its own way. Even in the story Jesus told about the prodigal son, the Father allowed the son to go, squander everything he had been given, and hit rock bottom. From the beginning God has allowed humans to make their own choices, and we see daily the effects of this. We're always puzzled by the common question, "Why would a good God send people to hell?" The real puzzle is why a just and good God would save people from the hell they have chosen, created on their own, and inflict on others even after He has warned them repeatedly about the consequences of their actions. The only answer is His great love and mercy.

So in light of these two amazing truths: God is willing to converse with us about what He is planning, and God has given to everyone, even our children, a free will to make their own choices, how should we pray?

START WITH PRAISE AND WORSHIP

It always starts here. Spend time worshiping your Savior and adoring Him. Call out His great attributes. We could do this just because He is infinitely worthy of it, but something amazing happens when we focus on His greatness. It sets our hearts in the right place. One of our kids once asked us if it was prideful or wrong for God to expect us to worship Him. Our response was to remind them of our recent trip to Yosemite. While hiking through those majestic mountains, would it have been wrong for them to ask us to notice them? If we were doing nothing but looking at the pavement, would it have been prideful of Yosemite Falls to ask us to look up at its beauty? Of course not! If we never looked at the grandeur of Half Dome or El Capitan, we would miss so much, and the park would have no effect on us.

God is much more captivating than even Yosemite. When we lift our eyes up to His beauty, we are changed. When we remind ourselves of His power, love, mercy, etc., our hearts begin to realign where they should be and where our prayers need to originate from, an attitude of faith and confidence in our great God.

"Our Father in heaven, hallowed be your name" (Matthew 6:9).

"Rejoice in the Lord always. I will say it again: Rejoice! Let your gentleness be evident to all. The Lord is near. Do not be anxious about anything, but in every situation, by prayer and petition, with thanksgiving, present your requests to God. And the peace of God, which transcends all understanding, will guard your hearts and your minds in Christ Jesus" (Philippians 4:4–7).

REPENT

As we mentioned in the previous chapter, repentance is a way of life for a Christian. Please don't mistake this with getting re-saved every time you pray or sin. The blood of Jesus covered your sins—past, present, and future—as soon as you repented of your lifestyle of sin and committed to following Him as Lord and Savior. If you have asked for forgiveness of your sins, want Jesus to be your Lord, and spend time remaining in Him, you are saved. You will mess up sometimes, for sure, but that does not mean you have lost your salvation. Similar to worship, repentance causes a positive change in us and aligns our hearts where they should be. We are in agreement with God that sin is sin, and any sin we have committed is wrong. Sin is such a dangerous cancer to the soul that we want to identify it and admit it before God as soon as possible, so that, in cooperation with the Holy Spirit, we can get it out of our lives before it does any more damage.

You may need to repent of sins against the child you're praying for. We will discuss that in more detail in chapter 9. However, you do not need to keep repenting of past sins. God wants to forgive you so badly that He sent His Son to die for it. Your sins are forgiven. Carrying on a habit of repentance for any sin you've committed that day isn't getting you in better standing with God. He already sees all the righteousness of Jesus when He looks at you.

When Jesus washed His disciples' feet, Peter wanted Him to wash his hands and head too. Jesus responded that Peter was already clean; he only needed his feet washed. Sometimes we walk in places we shouldn't and get a bit messy. We're still saved; we just need a little cleanup. By coming into agreement with God about what is sin, admitting when we do it, and asking for the Holy Spirit's help to keep from doing it again, we are keeping ourselves from dangerous places.

After giving us examples of people who have shown great faith in God, the writer of Hebrews tells us, "Therefore, since we are surrounded by such a great cloud of witnesses, let us throw off everything that hinders and the sin that so easily entangles. And let us run with perseverance the race marked out for us, fixing our eyes on Jesus, the pioneer and perfecter of faith" (Hebrews 12:1–2).

ASK FOR THE HOLY SPIRIT'S LEADING

Some believers are a bit freaked out by the Holy Spirit. Let us assure you, you need Him. How many of us would love it if Jesus were still here physically on earth. Seriously, sign us up for an evening with Jesus. We could ask Him all our questions and get wisdom for specific situations. We would, no doubt, be strengthened and encouraged just by spending time with Him. The problem is that when Jesus was here in the flesh, He allowed Himself to be limited by His flesh. He was only in one place at a time. There are 7.8 billion people on our planet right now. That's a lot of dinner appointments for Jesus.

In John 16:7–15, Jesus says:

> But very truly I tell you, it is for your good that I am going away. Unless I go away, the Advocate will not come to you; but if I go, I will send him to you. When he comes, he will prove the world to be in the wrong about sin and righteousness and judgement. . . . I have much more to say to you, more than you can now bear. But when he, the Spirit of truth, comes, he will guide you into all the truth. He will not speak on his own; he will speak only what he hears, and he will tell you what is yet to come. He will glorify me because it is from me that he will receive what he will make known to you. All that belongs to the Father is mine. That is why I said the Spirit will receive from me what he will make known to you.

Those who are in Christ receive the blessing of the Holy Spirit, and it's like having dinner with Jesus! He really will lead, guide, instruct, and comfort you just as if Jesus Himself was in the room, because they are one.

In Luke 11:9–13, Jesus tells us:

> Ask and it will be given to you; seek and you will find; knock and the door will be opened to you. For everyone who asks receives; the one who seeks finds; and to the one who knocks, the door will be opened. Which of you fathers, if your son asks for a fish, will give him a snake instead? Or if he asks for an egg, will give him a scorpion? If you then, though you are evil, know how to give good gifts to your children, how much more will your Father in heaven give the Holy Spirit to those who ask him!

What does this look like in real life? A few years ago I (Diana) had a very detailed dream about our prodigal child. I woke up fully believing that this dream was from God. I simultaneously felt a strong desire to take our child on a trip to Chicago. I ran everything past Jeff and he agreed. While in the Windy City, a bus we were on pulled up to an area that looked exactly like a place in my dream. Next thing we knew, we were unexpectedly stuck in a prayer meeting and spent two hours hashing out hurts and misunderstandings. Now I believed more than ever that the dream had been given to me by the Holy Spirit. The dream had other parts to it as well, and I have allowed them to change my heart and attitude toward my child while also guiding me in what to pray. That dream encourages me when I get tired of not seeing the results I want to see. I know God is working.

You need the Holy Spirit to give you specific guidance with your prodigal. Ask Him for His help **daily**, and He will be faithful to give it.

PRAY GOD'S WORD

Earlier, we mentioned a conversation that Abraham had with God. In that exchange, Abraham pointed out some of God's characteristics to God Himself to make his case stronger. How do we do what Abraham did? We pray God's own Word to Him. Oftentimes, we will declare to God that His Word tells us He doesn't show favoritism. We will recount back to God His encounter with Saul on the Damascus Road. We will ask him to have an encounter with our child as well.

We will write out Scriptures as prayers, as the Holy Spirit leads, and pray them each day both for our children and ourselves. Here is an example of what that looks like.

Recently, I (Diana) felt the Lord convicting me of being timid in some areas. I repented, but then I wrote out this prayer to pray each day to battle timidity in my life:

"It is written, according to 2 Timothy 1:6–9, that a spirit of fear is not from God. I bind, remove, and cast out any spirit of fear or timidity from working in my life, in Jesus's powerful name. I ask for the gifts that God has graciously given me to be fanned into a roaring flame for His glory. I ask that the Holy Spirit will operate in me and through me in power, love, and self-control. By the power of the Holy Spirit, I will not be ashamed of the testimony of my Lord or God's work in my life but will share in any suffering for the gospel by the power of God, who saved me and called me to a holy calling, not because of my works but because of His own purpose and grace in Christ Jesus."

If we read a Scripture that we believe applies to something one of our children is walking through, we will write it out, applying it to them personally like in the above example, and pray it until we feel released to move on.

God really doesn't mind when we remind Him what He has already said about Himself and His affection, care, attitude, and love toward us and our children. When it's done in faith, trusting entirely in who His Word says He is, it is not only appropriate but powerful! At the end of this

RESTORE THE ROAD HOME

book, we will include some of our favorite Scriptures to pray for our children. Take the ones that speak to you and write out a personal prayer for you or your children.

BE WILLING TO ACCEPT DANGEROUS OR UNCOMFORTABLE ANSWERS

Do we really want our child to be knocked off a horse and struck blind by God like Saul? No. But we want whatever it takes to cause repentance, and that might not be pretty. It was dangerous and uncomfortable for the father to allow the prodigal son to go off on his own with wealth in his pocket and rebellion in his heart. None of us want our children to end up hungry and filthy in a pig pen. But that was what it took for the prodigal to come to his senses.

When to the father's delight the prodigal returned home, other problems were created. Prodigals can be messy and may have issues or relationship complications that come home with them.

The mission statement at our church is "Mosaic Church exists to bring the prodigals home." That is not only our mission but the prayer and desire of our hearts. We long to see those who have lived apart from God come home to His kiss and loving embrace. We long to be a church who runs hard alongside the Father to meet those who are coming home.

Recently we attended a conference for pastors. The speaker threw out the idea that some of us don't really want the things we are praying for. We think we want them, but in reality, we want an idealized version of them. While listening to him, we were reminded of a couple in our church who are newly saved. They make us a little crazy sometimes. The drama they create is just so, well, immature. It dawned on us that when we pray for hundreds of prodigals to come home to our church, we are asking God for many more couples just like that and all the drama that comes with them.

We were babysitting our grandson a few nights ago, and when it came time to feed him dinner, he created a mess. He got potatoes everywhere! Potatoes on his clothes, potatoes on our clothes, potatoes on the floor, even potatoes on our phones. We didn't resent him for it. We cleaned him (and ourselves) up and continued feeding him. Babies make messes, and that is true physically and spiritually. As we are praying dangerous prayers for our children, we need to also ask God to prepare our own hearts to receive the answers to those prayers with grace, wisdom, love, and patience.

FASTING

We're not going to reveal who is who, but one of us is great at fasting and the other one acts like she is dramatically languishing on a fainting couch. Fasting is hard. It's made a bit harder because there is usually not an immediate reward for depriving yourself. However, if you are serious about prayer, you should be fasting.

In 2 Samuel 24:24 King David is going to offer a sacrifice to the Lord. Araunah offers to give him what he needs, but David's response is, "I will not sacrifice to the Lord my God burnt offerings that cost me nothing." Don't mistake what we're saying here: fasting is not paying God to answer your prayer, but it is showing God that you are willing to pay a price for the answer.

Fasting also empowers us over the enemy. Our own flesh and desires are powerful tools the enemy can twist and use for his own purposes. When we willingly refrain from one of our most basic and important needs for a time, we weaken Satan's ability to use our physical longings against us.

In Daniel 10, Daniel has received a vision that troubles him greatly, so he fasts for twenty-one days and prays for wisdom. The answer is given immediately, but the angel bringing it is detained in battle against a demonic force. The angel Michael comes to his aid, and he is finally able to deliver the message to Daniel. Scripture doesn't necessarily lay out

RESTORE THE ROAD HOME

how, but it does make it clear that fasting breaks demonic strongholds and aids in spiritual victories.

If the only reason we fast is because Jesus told us to, that is reason enough. "When [not if] you fast, do not look somber as the hypocrites do [get off the fainting couch], for they disfigure their faces to show others they are fasting. Truly I tell you, they have received their reward in full. But when you fast, put oil on your head and wash your face, so that it will not be obvious to others that you are fasting, but only to your Father, who is unseen; and your Father, who sees what is done in secret, will reward you" (Matthew 6:16–18).

Feel free to get creative with fasting. Some people fast from all food or from different types of food. Some fast from sunup to sundown. Others fast from something other than food such as TV or social media.

In John 15, Jesus tells us to remain in Him. Prayer, worship, and obeying the Word is how we do that. Then our Savior gives us this amazing promise that when we remain in Him, we can "ask whatever we wish, and it will be done for us" to the Father's glory and we will bear much fruit. Isn't that what we want? Prayer is the key. It isn't complicated. It really is having a conversation with God. When your heart is wanting to love Him, honor Him, and appeal for His help, you won't go wrong.

CHAPTER 6

LET'S FIGHT

There is something you should know about us. We are big fans of superhero movies. Really, what's not to love about someone with superpowers defending the weak and defeating the bad guy? We've seen a lot of them, and they so often follow in the same vein. A hero is found in an unexpected place. There is a villain who seems too powerful to defeat. Our hero typically gets knocked down a few times and may even become discouraged. People almost always underestimate him or her. Finally there's an epic battle where it looks like the good guy may not win, but strength and power are found right when all looks bleak, and evil is conquered. Although this story has been told in various forms over and over for millennia, it really has its origin in heaven. This is God's story. He is the one who has put this story in the hearts and imaginations of mankind.

We long for the beauty of that story, so we create and recreate it over and over again with different characters. C. S. Lewis said, "Now the story of Christ is simply a true myth: a myth working on us the same way as the others, but with this tremendous difference that it really happened: and one must be content to accept it in the same way, remembering that it is God's myth where the others are men's myth: i.e., the Pagan stories are God expressing Himself through the minds of poets, using such images as He found there, while Christianity is God expressing Himself through what we call 'real things.'" In other words, the astonishing, supernatural story of Christ is actually true. Throughout history, our superhero stories or myths have been birthed from the longing for a hero that God instilled in the minds of men.

Jesus is the only one who lived this story perfectly, but we can find teachable lessons in the manmade pictures that some of these stories give us. There is a scene in the movie *Wonder Woman* that we particularly love.

Without endorsing everything in the movie, we'll give you a basic snapshot in case you haven't seen it. It's set during World War I. Diana (aka Wonder Woman) is trying to track down Ares, the god of war, to stop him and this horrible world conflict. She has the help of Steve, an American spy. Diana isn't just anyone, by the way; she is the daughter of Zeus, created to take on Ares.

Diana and Steve end up at the front lines of battle where they cannot move forward because the enemy has a stronghold. There is an area called "no man's land" that cannot be crossed because the gunfire from the Germans on the other side is too great. The army has been stuck here for weeks. While Steve is looking for a way to go back, Diana is stopped by a distraught woman. Her village is on the other side. The enemy has captured it and enslaved the men, women, and children. The people are starving, she tells Diana as she begs for help.

Steve and the other soldiers refuse, not because they don't care, they do; it's just that the enemy is too strong, and crossing "no man's land" is humanly impossible. Ahh, but Diana knows something they don't. She has superpowers. She dons her sword and shield and steps into the line of fire. And boy does the fire come. At first it's just a bullet or two. That's a piece of cake for Wonder Woman. She deflects them easily. However, the Germans have developed machine guns by now, and they begin to unleash their full force. By the time she gets halfway across, all Wonder Woman can do is hold up her shield and defend herself against the nonstop barrage. The fire is too great for her to advance, until Steve and the other soldiers see what is happening. They grab their guns and run over the barricades to provide cover and return fire for Diana to advance.

As they work together and take full advantage of Wonder Woman's superpowers, they defeat a powerful enemy and set free the captives on the other side. We are not ashamed to admit that we teared up during this scene as we watched a movie give life to what a real spiritual battle must look like.

So here is our question for you: do you believe that you have superpowers?

You see, we mentioned that Jesus is the only one who did this hero thing perfectly, and that's true. But Jesus also said, "Very truly I tell you, whoever believes in me will do the works I have been doing, and they will do even greater things than these, because I am going to the Father. And I will do whatever you ask in my name, so that the Father may be glorified in the Son. You may ask me for anything in my name, and I will do it" (John 14:12–14).

He also said, "I will build my church, and the gates of Hades will not overcome it. I will give you the keys of the kingdom of heaven; whatever you bind on earth will be bound in heaven, and whatever you loose on earth will be loosed in heaven" (Matthew 16:18–19).

Wait, there's more. "Truly I tell you, if you have faith and do not doubt, not only can you do what was done to the fig tree [Jesus had ordered it to never bear fruit again, and the tree immediately withered], but also you can say to this mountain, 'Go, throw yourself into the sea,' and it will be done. If you believe, you will receive whatever you ask for in prayer" (Matthew 21:21–22).

If you are a disciple of Jesus, you have been given supernatural powers by your Master. You, my friend, are a superhero.

As people who spend a lot of time in church, we can hear Scriptures like these so often that they almost become white noise. We quote them to one another ("The devil prowls around like a roaring lion"), and some we even put on mugs or paintings ("We wrestle not against flesh and blood"). We can't allow the familiarity of some passages of Scripture to cause them to lose their strength and urgency. We are in a dangerous, serious battle, and it is time to use our God-given supernatural power and fight back.

In the last chapter we talked about how to pray effectively. There is a difference between spiritual warfare and prayer. We pray to our loving Father. We battle our cunning enemy. In this chapter we will go to battle. The two often go hand in hand, but their purpose and direction are different. The purpose of spiritual warfare is to detect the schemes of our enemy and defeat him and his work. Sounds kind of like war. The purpose of prayer is to commune with God, give Him praise, hear His heart, and present our requests to our loving Father.

So now, let's put on our capes and jump into some fundamental truths about the battle we are about to engage in with a supervillain to rescue those he has taken captive.

TRUTH #1: THE BATTLE IS REAL

We discussed Peter's failures in the last chapter. Prior to those, one of the warnings Jesus gave Peter was that Satan had asked to sift him like wheat (Luke 22:31). Some translations say that Satan demanded, asserted the right, or asked excessively. It's pretty clear that Satan was after Peter. Years later, a more mature, wise, and seasoned Peter said, "Be alert and of sober mind. Your enemy the devil prowls around like a roaring lion looking for someone to devour" (1 Peter 5:8). Peter had learned some things the hard way.

What did Satan mean by asking to sift the disciples like wheat? Satan wanted to show what they were made of. A kernel of wheat is valuable. It can be eaten as food or planted to produce more wheat. It can be kind of difficult to separate it from the chaff, which isn't of value. We can't eat or plant the chaff. Wheat is heavier, so by repeatedly throwing the wheat and chaff up in the wind (a process called winnowing), the chaff will eventually all blow away, leaving the valuable wheat. Satan was essentially calling Peter's bluff. Peter thought he was wheat. Satan was willing to bet that he was chaff. Satan believed Peter was worthless, something that would just blow away in the wind.

The devil was correct about one thing: Peter did crumble under the scrutiny. Where Satan got it very wrong was in thinking that Peter's value and worth to Jesus rested in Peter's ability to get it right all the time. Peter was of great value because he belonged to Jesus, period. Peter was wheat, not chaff. You are wheat, not because of who you are but because of Whose you are. Jesus wants you. And because Jesus wants you, Satan hates you.

We once heard a pastor describe a counseling session with a lady who hated her husband. During the meeting she took a picture of her husband out of her purse and ripped it into tiny pieces. Why would she do that? Because her husband was stronger than she was. She couldn't actually do any physical damage to him. All she could do was take out her rage on his image. Satan can't do a thing to God. Death is Satan's most powerful weapon, and even that failed against God. All he can do now is try to tear into the image of God—us. Remember your new name, "little Christ"?

How does he do that? Satan is not omnipotent, which means all-powerful, and he is not omnipresent, which means all-places. Only God is omnipotent and omnipresent. Lucifer (aka Satan, the devil) is a single being who can only be in one place at a time. In that way, he has the same limits as any created being. Yes, he is limited, but he is also, according to Scripture, cunning and sly. He has demons (or fallen angels) who have aligned themselves with him. It's naive of us to think that Lucifer hasn't set up those under his command just like any other commander who wants to overthrow a power. When Ephesians 6 tells us that our struggle is "not against flesh and blood," it means that we are not in a fight with other humans. Paul goes on to say in that chapter that we are in a fight with "**rulers**, against the **authorities**, against the **powers** of this dark world and against the **spiritual forces of evil** in the heavenly realms." Satan exists. Demons exist. They have powers, authority, and rule. They function as a force similar to any military unit.

We would go so far as to say that Lucifer himself probably doesn't even know who we are. If we know anything about him, we know that he is grandiose in his thinking about himself, which means that he probably doesn't make time for the likes of a pastor and pastor's wife in a small California city. He doesn't need to know we exist because he has other "spiritual forces of evil" to advance his will. Who do you think those "spiritual forces of evil" concern themselves with? Yep, their focus is followers of Christ. We would bet that some of those rulers, authorities, powers, and spiritual dark forces know who you are and who we are.

The historical book of Acts recounts the fascinating story of some sons of a Jewish priest named Sceva. In Acts 19:13–16 we read that Paul was driving out demons. Why was Paul driving out demons? Because Paul was a follower of Jesus, and as a follower of Jesus he had authority and power over any evil spirit. Seven of Sceva's sons decided they would like that power too. Problem was, they didn't know Jesus—they just knew Paul. They tried to drive a demon out of a man by saying, "In the name of the Jesus whom Paul preaches, I command you to come out." The demon spoke to the men and said, "Jesus I know, and Paul I know about, but who are you?" This evil spirit didn't need to concern himself with anyone who didn't have power. You have power. Evil spirits will concern themselves with you.

In 2019 we visited New Orleans for the first time with some friends. The architecture was beautiful, and the beignets were delicious! We had a good time, but there was definitely a spiritual heaviness in that city. One day while walking near Jackson Square, we ended up on a street with booths for fortune tellers and tarot card and palm readers. Knowing that demons are at work in these things, we wondered if they took any notice of us as we walked by. I (Jeff) was the pastor of those in the group. That night I had a nightmare of one of my children horrifically committing suicide in front of me. I've never had a nightmare like that before. If we were to peel back the curtain of the spiritual realm, we believe we would have seen that those evil spirits indeed noticed us. They even were able to distinguish who was the spiritual leader of the group and make me their target.

If any of this frightens you, please don't let it. **You have power and authority over demons.** Peter was wise to tell us to be alert and sober-minded about this stuff, but he did not tell us to be scared. We have no reason to fear because of our next fundamental truth.

TRUTH #2: JESUS HAS VICTORY OVER ALL POWERS OF DARKNESS

Colossians 2:10 tells us that Jesus is "the head over **every** power and authority." Then in verses 13–15 we are told that Jesus "forgave us all our sins, having canceled the charge of our legal indebtedness, which stood against us and condemned us; he has taken it away, nailing it to the cross. And having **disarmed the powers and authorities, he made a public spectacle of them, triumphing over them by the cross.**" Drop. The. Mic.

Jesus took care of more than our sins on the cross. Our Savior, who is to be forever praised, defeated and disarmed our powerful supervillain and his hordes. Not only that, He humiliated them in front of everyone.

The Message Bible (MSG) says it like this, "Think of it! All sins forgiven, the slate wiped clean, that old arrest warrant canceled and nailed to Christ's cross. He stripped all the spiritual tyrants in the universe of their sham authority at the Cross and marched them naked through the streets."

That's our superhero!

And as if canceling the charges against us and disarming and humiliating our enemy wasn't enough, He went ahead and shook off the shackles of death after slapping Satan around for a few days. In Revelation 1:18 Jesus says, "I am the Living One; I was dead, and now look, I am alive for ever and ever! And I hold the keys of death and Hades." When Jesus rose from the dead, He showed the world and the powers of darkness that their most powerful weapon can't do a thing against Him. Oh, and you know what? It just keeps getting better because that powerful weapon can't do a thing against us either! Our King holds those keys.

"Death has been swallowed up in victory. Where, O death, is your victory? Where, O death, is your sting? The sting of death is sin, and the power of sin is the law. But thanks be to God! He gives **us** the victory through our Lord Jesus Christ" (1 Corinthians 15:54–57).

Satan's strongest weapon didn't work on Jesus, and it doesn't work on us.

That's a whole lot of good news; however, let's take a look at our "buts" for a moment. We know that Jesus has victory over death, **but** this world we live in right now can serve up a whole lot of pain. We know that through Jesus we have authority and power over spiritual dark forces, **but** how do we actually use that power? This is all great for us, **but** what about my child who isn't a follower of Christ? This is all wonderful, **but** does being a follower of Jesus mean more than just having my sins forgiven and living eternally with God? Yes, it does.

TRUTH #3: JESUS GIVES HIS POWER AND AUTHORITY TO HIS FOLLOWERS

"These signs will accompany those who believe: In my name they will drive out demons; they will speak in new tongues; they will pick up snakes with their hands; and when they drink deadly poison, it will not hurt them at all; they will place their hands on sick people, and they will get well" (Mark 16:17–18).

Paul tells us in 2 Corinthians 10:3–4, "For though we live in the world, we do not wage war as the world does. The weapons we fight with are not the weapons of the world. On the contrary, they have **divine power** to demolish strongholds."

"I saw Satan fall like lightning from heaven. I have given you authority to trample on snakes and scorpions and to overcome all the power of the enemy; nothing will harm you. However, do not rejoice that the spirits submit to you, but rejoice that your names are written in heaven" (Luke 10:18–20).

In a way, this chapter is an extension of chapter 4 on our identity. We have to learn to walk and function in the powers that God has given us through Jesus Christ our Lord. A few months ago, a practicing witch started coming to the Sunday night prayer and worship meetings at our church. Her purpose was not to know Christ. Her purpose was to disrupt. She had a reputation for going around to different churches trying to cause trouble. The first night we met her, she asked us to pray for her daughter. Something was off, and after praying for her daughter, we began to talk to her about a relationship with Jesus. She informed us that she was a witch and had no interest in knowing Jesus. That didn't shock us because we had already sensed a spirit against God. We continued to chat with her until she finally asked us, "Why aren't you scared of me?"

What a ridiculous question. Us scared of her? In a nutshell, our response was, "No offense, but we have no reason to be scared of you. If we're talking about power, we are the ones with real power." She came to church a few more times, but she didn't get very far in her attempts to create havoc. The Holy Spirit revealed something to us that we were going to expose the next time she returned, but she stopped coming.

The whole thing was heartbreaking because she could have been set free if she would have surrendered to the one who loves her. But honestly, the other thing that grieved us was her assumption that Christians would be afraid of her. Her experience had been that when she threw around the word "witch," Christians trembled in fear. That should never be!

Our God is the one who enabled a boy to slay a giant with a slingshot. Our God is the one who demolished the walls of Jericho at a trumpet blast. Our God is the one who shut the mouths of lions for Daniel. Our God walked with Shadrach, Meshach, and Abednego in the fiery furnace. Our God parted the Red Sea. Our God healed the blind, deaf, lame, and leper. Our God punched death in the face and walked out of the grave. Our God equips the simple to function in wisdom and power. Our God takes ashes, tragedy, and heartbreak and brings beauty, purpose, and healing. Tell me, who do we need to be afraid of? We fear nobody and nothing.

The only one who should ever instill fear in us is God. "I tell you, my friends, do not be afraid of those who kill the body and after that can do no more. But I will show you whom you should fear: Fear him who, after your body has been killed, has authority to throw you into hell. Yes, I tell you, fear him." But even the terror of God melts away by the love of God. Jesus continues, "Are not five sparrows sold for two pennies? Yet not one of them is forgotten by God. Indeed, the very hairs of your head are all numbered. **Don't be afraid; you are worth more than many sparrows**" (Luke 12:4–7).

If you are a follower of Jesus, you are loved. You are given power and authority. You have superpowers for the purpose of battling a powerful enemy and setting captives free. You have nothing to fear.

So if we believe these truths, how do we actually function in them?

REMAIN IN CHRIST

We talked about this in the last chapter, and it is the most important aspect of spiritual warfare. In John 15:5–8, Jesus says, "I am the vine; you are the branches. If you remain in me and I in you, you will bear much fruit; apart from me you can do nothing. If you do not remain in me, you are like a branch that is thrown away and withers; such branches are picked up, thrown into the fire and burned. If you remain in me and my words remain in you, ask whatever you wish, and it will be done for you. This is to my Father's glory, that you bear much fruit, showing yourselves to be my disciples."

You can do nothing apart from Jesus. If you are not spending time with Him daily and throughout your day, expect to be weak and ineffective. Don't just spend time in the "God, I want a pony" prayers. Spend real time in His Word reading Scriptures that tell you who you are and how you should be living. When those Scriptures, like a mirror, show you where you fall short, spend time talking to God about it, confessing, and asking for His help to walk in obedience. Spend time asking Him what His heart is for specific situations, and then spend time pausing to listen. Please notice how often we used the word "time" in this paragraph. Are we telling you that you should actually be spending more time with God than watching Netflix? If you want to be effective and fruitful, then yes, we are. Your superpowers derive from one source. If you are not spending time with the source, you will not have power.

EMBRACE THE GIFTS OF THE SPIRIT

We were talking with a friend the other day who jokingly equated Catholics with the Father, Protestants with the Son, and charismatics with the Holy Spirit. He imagined God saying to His church, "Hey, we three all get along and function beautifully as one and so should you."

We've compartmentalized Christianity to the point that we have churches who focus on Scripture but won't allow the Holy Spirit to make a peep. The Bible is holy, correct, and true, but it is not part of the Trinity. The Holy Spirit is. How dare we attempt to muzzle Him and tell the gift Jesus gave us that He was done speaking at the end of Acts.

Then we have churches that allow anything and everything that seems "spiritual" because they love the excitement it brings. Or churches that assert that God indeed still speaks, but He's changed His mind about what is sin and what is not.

The Holy Spirit will not tell you that it's OK to do that thing you really want to do even though Scripture says it's wrong. The Holy Spirit will not put on a show so that people will be impressed and entertained. The Holy Spirit will give you specific wisdom, direction, guidance, and power for situations you find yourself dealing with.

> But when he, the Spirit of truth, comes, he will guide you into all the truth. He will not speak on his own; he will speak only what he hears, and he will tell you what is yet to come. He will glorify me because it is from me that he will receive what he will make known to you. (John 16:13–14)

> But you will receive power when the Holy Spirit comes on you; and you will be my witnesses in Jerusalem, and in all Judea and Samaria, and to the ends of the earth. (Acts 1:8)

> There are different kinds of gifts, but the same Spirit distributes them. There are different kinds of service, but the same Lord. There are different kinds of working, but in all of them and in everyone it is the same God at work. Now to each one the manifestation of the Spirit is given for the common good. To one there is given through the Spirit a message of wisdom, to another a message of knowledge by means of the same Spirit, to another faith by the same Spirit, to another gifts of healing by that one Spirit, to another miraculous powers, to another prophecy, to another distinguishing between spirits, to another speaking in different kinds of tongues, and to still another the interpretation of

tongues. All these are the work of one and the same Spirit, and he distributes them to each one, just as he determines. (1 Corinthians 12:4–11)

Unlike movie superheroes, we are not the ones who decide when and where to use our superpowers. As we remain in Christ and commune with God, we get to know His heart and will. Then the Holy Spirit distributes gifts for specific uses at specific times for His glory and the bearing of fruit. If you are engaging in battle without the gifts of the Holy Spirit, you are like a blindfolded man wildly swinging a sword. You have an effective weapon, but you can't see how to use it with accuracy and precision. It makes the battle more exhausting and discouraging than it should be.

I (Diana) had a rough labor with our first child. When the go-ahead to push finally came, I was more than ready to be done with all the pain and get that baby out. I pushed and pushed and pushed to no avail. My strength was almost spent, but I had made no progress whatsoever. A nurse came over and told me I was focusing on pushing in the wrong spot. She touched a specific area and said, "Push here." Voilà, like magic, my pushing and effort all of a sudden started accomplishing something. It actually took less of my own strength and effort when I focused on the right area. It was less draining and more effective.

When we allow the Holy Spirit to lead us into battle, we now have the all-powerful, all-knowing God telling us when to speak, when to keep silent, how to pray, when there is a spirit that needs to be bound and removed, when healing needs to take place, and in what area. And those are only a few things that begin to happen when we walk by the Spirit.

We'll give you an example of what that looks like in the real world. Years ago we were asked to take the lead role in an established ministry. We needed to know what the Lord wanted so we began to ask Him to lead us. It was during a vacation, while walking among ancient ruins, that Jeff heard the Lord speak to him and give him direction to go ahead and accept the position. When we got home from that trip, a friend contacted us saying that the Lord had awoken her in the middle of the night with a Scripture to give to us. It was out of Isaiah 58 and spoke about rebuilding the ancient ruins. How timely, and it gave us peace and confirmation that we had heard from God.

At the time we had no idea of the ruins that needed to be rebuilt. We knew that a lot needed to be done, though, so we got to work. A couple of months later, one of us was given a dream from the Lord about the ministry. We knew God was speaking but didn't quite know what it meant. We wrote it down and asked for clarity.

A few months later, amid our hardest season in ministry, there was another strange dream. Again, we didn't know exactly what it meant, but we wrote it down and asked for clarity. The dream proved to be prophetic as two days later we began receiving harassing phone calls. Over the next several months we were harassed on a regular basis, even in public.

While this was going on, a few things were happening. I (Diana) was having intrusive thoughts that were almost impossible to control. That's not normal for me, and I had never experienced anything like it. I also smacked my head, requiring a trip to urgent care to get a cut glued shut. Jeff had a freak accident that broke several bones and required two surgeries. The other, even stranger, thing that happened was that it seemed like everywhere we went, someone was talking about the "spirit of Jezebel." People who didn't even attend our church would all of a sudden pray against a spirit of Jezebel. At a brunch, one person from out of town started talking about the dangers of a spirit of Jezebel. We kept ignoring it. It was just coincidence. We believed in evil spirits but didn't think there was anything to naming one Jezebel or that we were battling it. Finally a trusted friend of ours, without knowing anything we were going through, shared a video of someone speaking about how to know if you are being harassed by a spirit of Jezebel. Out of curiosity, we watched it. Just about everything he listed was happening in our lives, including intrusive thoughts and strange accidents.

So we prayed. We prayed for wisdom and protection and honestly told the Lord we didn't know what to do.

One day a woman who often prayed for us felt the Holy Spirit direct her to share some insight. As she drove to meet with us, she felt a strong pressure on her chest that was almost unbearable. Once she arrived, the pressure went away. She began sharing things that the Lord had revealed years before that spoke to our current situation. As we prayed together, she prayed words that directly corelated to one of the dreams that we had, even though we hadn't shared the dream with her. She confirmed that we were dealing with an evil spirit.

We know, it's weird. It's a bit creepy. What do you do with all of that? We are people of faith. We do not believe there is a demon behind everything, but we also don't believe in coincidences. We felt we had been shown enough that not to take action would be walking in disobedience. We called together a few people who know how to pray and told them everything. We anointed every room in the ministry with oil and prayed over it. We took the authority and power God has given us and told the spirit that was harassing us and our ministry that it could do so no more. We didn't care if its name was Jezebel or anything else— it had to go. Do you know what happened? It left because it had to. The harassing calls stopped. The intrusive thoughts stopped. There were no more accidents. But the better thing that happened was that we grew in wisdom and discernment. Not every intrusive thought or accident is the result of spiritual warfare, but some are, and you need to be able to discern the voice of the Holy Spirit to know the difference. The Holy Spirit spoke to us through dreams, prophecies, Scripture, words of knowledge, and wisdom given to us and others so that we were able to battle a specific spirit that was causing trouble.

The last way that we function in the above truths is that at some point we have to actually . . .

ENGAGE IN BATTLE

We recounted that story to show you what engaging in warfare can look like when you're dealing with an evil spirit. What does that have to do with our kids who have rejected Christ? Everything! While it's true that we cannot use the power God gives us to force them into relationship with God (nor would we want to—control is not love), 2 Corinthians 4:4 tells us, "The god of this age has blinded the minds of unbelievers, so that they cannot see the light of the gospel that displays the glory of Christ, who is the image of God." We can battle the one who wants to keep them blinded to truth and headed for destruction. That takes listening to the Spirit of God and obeying Him, even when it feels uncomfortable.

The above story wrapped up nicely by the end. The battle we are fighting for our prodigal is ongoing. God has directed us. The Holy Spirit has spoken to us in dreams and words of knowledge from others. He has given us opportunities to speak and told us to be quiet at times. We are still fighting, and so we are trusting that He is still leading, even when we get tempted to take over.

If you have a sense that there are demonic strongholds in your child's life, come against them. Make their work miserable because you are stripping them every day of their power to deceive your child. We want to be clear. We are not telling you that your child is possessed or that you have to cast out a demon. What we are saying is that there are evil spirits who work to trick, blind, and destroy the ones God loves. Children are a gift from the Lord. Something wants to steal your gift. Put up a fight. Your child still has a free will and can reject God, but I want to make sure there is no enemy of God tricking my child into believing a lie. The enemy is relentless in his attacks on our children. We need to be just as relentless in our attacks on his work in their lives.

There are different levels of demonic influence that can affect a person's life. Mild demonic influence is what happened to us in New Orleans.

Just like we can encounter a bully or a predator in the natural, we encountered a demon who tried to spiritually bully Jeff.

The person who harassed us is an example of moderate demonic influence. There was an open door that allowed a spirit to strongly influence someone, and that spirit needed to be removed.

Severe demonic influence is usually called possession. It is when someone is completely controlled by the evil spirit and considered its home. In cases of moderate or severe demonic influence it is wise to get help in prayer from your pastor and others who have been placed in church authority. If you would like more information on demonic influence, we would suggest books by Gil Stieglitz or Jake Kail.

As you battle, remember that you fight from a place of victory, not for victory. It's a subtle but important difference.

After the American colonies won the Revolutionary War, a new nation was born. You would think that the British, being defeated, went back home and left the Americans alone, but that's not what happened. The British continued to harass the new country and its citizens. One of the ways they did this was called impressment. They would stop American ships at sea, accuse the sailors of desertion, and force them into the Royal Navy.

Finally, the United States had had enough. During the presidency of James Madison, we engaged in battle again, even though we had already won. During the War of 1812, we had to once again flex our power against an already defeated foe.

In the same way, Satan continues to harass and try to enslave those who he truly has no power over. You fight him, yes, but through Christ, you fight him from the place of a victor. Because of Jesus, Satan and his kingdom are outsmarted, outgunned, outnumbered, and outpowered. Let's remind him of that truth!

A PRAYER YOU CAN PRAY

Heavenly Father, we are so grateful for the gifts you give us. You have gifted us our children, you have gifted us your Holy Spirit, and you have gifted us power and authority over the enemy. Thank you that we have nothing to fear because you have saved us from true danger through Jesus, and you have equipped us to fight for your cause and your glory. Now, in the name of Jesus, we come against any spirit that would set itself against you, Lord God, and seek to harm and deceive our child. We bind any evil spirit working in the life of our child and render that work impotent. In Jesus's name, we drive back any evil spirit from our child so that its lies cannot be heard. Holy Spirit, we ask that you would open our child's ears and eyes to hear truth and see truth.

CHAPTER 7

BE ALL IN FOR THE LONG HAUL

We sometimes joke that our motto is "We won't quit, even if we're crawling." It's not super inspirational, is it? We're not sure it'll sell a lot of books or ever be printed on a T-shirt or coffee mug, but it's the reality that most of us have to walk (or crawl) through at times.

When our child came to us with that conversation back in chapter 1, if faith were a person, ours got knocked down. A punch came out of nowhere, and our faith took one on the jaw. But our faith is strong and we got back up. We did more than get back up—we got back up ready to fight. And we fought. We took more blows. We fought some more. We took more blows. We would think we were about to see a victory, then something would knock us down again. It started to get discouraging.

We're '80s kids and grew up cheering for Rocky at the movies. In *Rocky IV*, Rocky is fighting the evil Soviet boxer Ivan Drago during the height of the Cold War. Drago is bigger, stronger, has more advanced training equipment, and takes steroids. Drago has already killed the former heavyweight champ, Apollo Creed, in the boxing ring, and now Rocky is taking him on. Rocky takes blow after blow after blow. In a jump-out-of-your-seat-worthy scene during the fight, Drago says, about Rocky, "He's not human. He is iron." During the boxing match, Rocky has fallen. He's stumbled. He's been hurt, dazed, and confused, but he just won't quit. Rocky beats Drago on his own turf.

The saga continues years later in the *Creed* movies. Apollo Creed's son, Adonis, is now the heavyweight champ under Rocky's coaching. Guess who comes to call? Ivan Drago with his son Viktor. Viktor challenges Adonis to a fight and gives him the most brutal beating he's ever experienced. However, since Viktor didn't fight fair, he is disqualified and Adonis remains the champ. Viktor wants a rematch and Adonis is scared. But Rocky knows what to do this time. He trains Adonis to take the pain. Rocky knows that fighting Viktor Drago will cause a lot of pain, and the young Creed will never win if that pain keeps him down.

You have an enemy who will inflict pain on you. With every blow, his desire is for you to stay down on the mat because he knows that if you keep getting back up and reentering the fight, his defeat is imminent. Like any champion boxer, we need to increase our stamina and pain tolerance if we're going to win.

Before we build our own stamina, let's take a look at some of the legends of the faith who built theirs. We've already talked about Abraham and the faith it took to believe God when days turned into years and years into decades. What about David? He was anointed and held the promise of being king of Israel. Then everything started going wrong. He was rejected, hunted, and slandered. He had to flee the country he was anointed king over to go live in a foreign land. Even when he did finally ascend to the throne, he had to deal with constant turmoil. Without all of that pain, we wouldn't have many of the psalms that have brought hope to countless people for millennia.

Joseph was given prophetic dreams of success and leadership. Then he ended up betrayed by his own family, sold into slavery, falsely accused of rape, and imprisoned. He sat in prison for twelve years, forgotten even by a fellow prisoner who had been set free. Waiting is normal for

God's people. We would even go so far as to say that waiting in dire circumstances is normal for God's people.

If God loves us, why does He make us wait? That famous, frustrating, difficult verse in James gives us the answer. "Consider it pure joy, my brothers and sisters, whenever you face trials of many kinds, because you know that the testing of your faith produces **perseverance. Let perseverance finish its work so that you may be mature and complete, not lacking anything**" (James 1:2–4).

God is more interested in a complete work than a quick fix. God wants us to be mature and complete and not lack anything we need for the plans and purposes He has for us. We are the ones who long for shortcuts. We were in the drive-through line at Chick-fil-A today. When the line split into two, we picked the one we hoped would be quickest. There was a nerve-racking moment when we thought we may have picked the wrong line and the other one would have been faster. We weren't in a particular hurry, but it was frustrating to think that the route we took might require more time to get us to our chicken sandwiches. If we are that impatient for **fast** food, imagine how impatient we are to see the things we have longed and prayed for come to pass, especially if there is pain involved in the waiting process.

Interestingly, prior to that conversation in chapter 1, we had noticed some little seeds of rebellion in our child. Nothing major, but things that needed to be rooted out. We began to pray that God would address those things. Oftentimes, we want the situation addressed without the mess it might make. It's as if we see that there are weeds. We want to pull the weeds up, but roots are ugly and pulling them out makes a mess. Sometimes we are tempted to believe that it's just easier to cover those weeds with dirt instead of going through the pain of rooting them out.

The thing is, God is a much more patient gardener than we are. He will tear up the whole garden, if He has to, to get to the root of those weeds and get them out of there. And you know what, He is not stressed about the temporary mess it makes. What if we really believed that God was purposeful in what He does and that, when the garden of your child's life (or yours) is being dug up and looks horrible, God is getting at those roots?

God will go to great lengths to make sure that our (and our child's) faith is mature, complete, and not lacking anything, because He loves us. In John 11:1–45, we find the story of Lazarus. We are all pretty familiar with the story, but there are a few things we want to take particular notice of. First of all, Jesus was purposeful in His timing. Jesus knew Lazarus was sick, yet He waited two days before He went to Judea. "Now Jesus loved Martha and her sister and Lazarus. **So** when he heard that Lazarus was sick, he stayed where he was two more days." He let Lazarus die on purpose because He loved them and was more interested in the maturity of their faith than their momentary pain. God is not afraid of dead things. You may be terrified right now that your child's marriage, career, legacy, relationships, dreams, or a myriad of other things might die while they are running from God. Some of those fears may come to pass, but remember this: God can make dead things come back to life. It's a wonder and a miracle, but that doesn't make it less true. God is willing to let something die so that His power can be made known and our faith (and our child's) can be complete.

When Jesus finally does arrive on the scene, He has two emotions—He is both compassionate and troubled. His compassion is evident in the shortest verse in the Bible: "Jesus wept." Jesus is willing to let Lazarus die. Jesus also knows that He is going to bring life to the situation and there will be a ripple effect of faith built in people. Those two things do not negate the fact that Jesus is compassionate and weeps because those He loves are in pain. Don't ever think that God's willingness to allow hard things keeps Him from being heartbroken with you for the pain those things cause. Jesus wept with those who were hurting even though He allowed it and was going to do something about it. This is the easiest verse in the Bible to memorize. Remind yourself of it when you experience the pain of dead things, and know that Jesus is weeping with you.

Jesus also felt troubled. Some translations say that He was angry. Why would He be angry at their lack of faith during this sorrowful time? Because it was a lack of faith in Him and His love, power, and character. Friends, Jesus is all we've got. Every other hope will fail us. If we can't have faith in Jesus during our worst-case scenarios, then we have nothing. Cling to it and don't let it go at any cost. Even if it sounds foolish to the whole world, in your darkest days, declare that your God can bring life to dead things.

In the words of David, "To you, O Lord, I lift up my soul. O my God, in you I trust; let me not be put to shame; let not my enemies exult over me. Indeed, none who wait for you shall be put to shame" (Psalm 25:1–3 ESV).

Writing this chapter is timely for us. We just received devastating news two days ago that something very dear to us might die. Along with it, other dreams would die too. We sat with one who was weeping, reminding them of these truths, and then we reminded ourselves. God could choose to save that thing before it dies, as Jesus did over and over in Scripture. God could choose to allow the death and resurrect it like He did Lazarus. Or God could choose to allow the death and restore life back to this situation in a different way, as He did with Job. If we put our faith in a particular outcome, we are doomed. We are certainly praying that God heals the situation before it's over. But our faith, peace, and hope are fixated on God and not which action He chooses to take.

As we're waiting on God's timing and His decisions, how do we preserve our stamina as the punches keep coming? Remember, we have an enemy who is relentless. We always tell our Battle Cry groups that things often will get worse before they get better. How do we stay in the fight?

Expect a Come-to-Jesus Moment in God's Timing, Not Yours

As you are praying for your child, waiting on God's timing, and trusting Him, you will be led by the Holy Spirit. It's tempting to discount God's work in your child's life because a conversation or encounter that you **know** was orchestrated by God didn't end with the result you wanted. In chapter 5 we told you about a dream and a God-orchestrated conversation that followed. Even though there was not a dramatic come-to-Jesus moment after that conversation, God was still in it, so we can trust that He had a purpose for it.

We have a dear friend who our children love. She has a testimony that she felt led by the Holy Spirit to share with our child who is running from God. She was praying. We were praying. The two of them met for dinner, and we were anxious to hear how it went. Hours passed. They had to be done by now, we thought. We finally texted, and she just responded that she would tell us about it the next day. Come to find out, it had gone really well. Our child loved and appreciated the intimacy of hearing her story and sincerely thanked her for sharing. But there was no repentance or turning to Jesus from our child, so our friend felt that she had failed. She was afraid to tell us. But she did not fail. She accomplished exactly what the Lord had prepared for her to accomplish.

"I [Paul] planted the seed, Apollos watered it, but God has been making it grow. So neither the one who plants nor the one who waters is anything, but only God, who makes things grow. The one who plants and the one who waters have one purpose, and they will each be rewarded according to their own labor" (1 Corinthians 3:6–8).

When the Israelites were ready to follow Joshua into the promised land, they had to conquer dozens of cities and battle multiple kings, and it took years. Each battle was an important victory to get them to the fulfillment of God's promise, but one battle didn't get the job done.

Don't get discouraged when one battle (or two, or five, or ten) doesn't win the war. Keep going.

Stop Needing Things to Be Perfect

Dear ones, we are not living in our eternal home yet. Perfect is coming and we can't wait! But perfect isn't here yet and it's hard. As we write this, we have just celebrated Mother's Day. As I (Diana) was gearing up for it, I thought about that devastating news we had just received and how it would keep this Mother's Day from being perfect. For a moment I was tempted to spiral into the lie that I couldn't enjoy my day of celebrating because there would be this black spot on it. But you see, my Savior has already prewarned me that I would have trouble in this world. He also declared that I can "take heart" during that trouble because He has overcome the world. I adjusted my attitude and thoroughly enjoyed my day.

You may never have a perfect Mother's Day or Christmas or birthday, but that doesn't mean you can't have good ones. However, you will never enjoy the good if you need the perfect. You'll never have a perfect year or season or week. Maybe, once in a blue moon, you'll have a day when everything just goes right. Thank God for that day, but know that it is an anomaly.

When we are in Christ, good days should be the norm. Not because they go off without a hitch but because we don't receive our joy, peace, and hope from perfect circumstances but from our perfect Savior who has promised never to leave or forsake us. A day of bad events can still be a day to praise Him because we have the confidence that He can work **all** things together for our good (Romans 8:28).

In her book *The Hiding Place*, Corrie ten Boom tells the story of when she and her sister Betsie arrived at the Ravensbrück concentration camp during WWll. As Corrie climbed into her bunk for the first time, she jumped up (bumping her head on the bunk above) and scurried out as fast as she could because it was infested with fleas. In despair, she asked her sister Betsie how they could live in a place like this. Betsie excitedly pulled out the Bible they had smuggled in and pointed out the verse they had read that very morning. "Rejoice always, pray continually, give thanks in **all** circumstances; for this is God's will for you in Christ Jesus" (1 Thessalonians 5:16–18).

Betsie insisted that they do just what the Scripture told them to do. They began to thank God that they were together. They rejoiced that He miraculously allowed them to smuggle a Bible in with them. When Betsie thanked God for the fleas, Corrie exclaimed that she had gone too far. Finally, with Betsie's prodding, Corrie reluctantly thanked God for the fleas.

As the weeks passed, the sisters noticed that the guards never came into the building where they were staying. In the temporary barracks, the guards were constantly patrolling. Here in their permanent dwelling, even though there were 1,400 women in there, the guards never stepped through the door. This allowed Corrie and Betsie to hold Bible studies twice a day for the women who were imprisoned with them. One day they needed a guard to help someone who was hurt, but the guard's response was, "I'm not going in there. It's infested with fleas." The fleas were a blessing that allowed women in the most brutal circumstances to have the truth of God's Word spoken into their lives each day.

We really can thank God in all circumstances.

Believe God Is Moving Even When You Can't See It

He is God, and that means we don't always see or know everything He's doing. I (Diana) had a short stint of running from God when I was nineteen. I had become friends with a group of really cool people, and I wanted to be really cool too. One of the girls in the group was a bit older and did tarot card readings. I wanted her to like me. I knew to stay away from things like tarot cards, but I was throwing off the "shackles" of all those "religious superstitions" and doing what I wanted. I kept asking her to tell my fortune, but she avoided me like the plague. It got to the point that she would shut herself in her bedroom whenever I was there hanging out with her roommates. I finally asked a mutual friend what was going on and was told, "She doesn't like being near you. She says you have bad karma." I have often wondered what was going on in the spiritual realm during that time.

Never forget that God is the one who sets the parameters of our wanderings. We truly believe that whatever bondage or open door to the enemy that would have resulted had I dabbled in occult activities was unnecessary for my ultimately coming back to Christ. We believe God simply said no and wouldn't allow it.

The questions surrounding how God's sovereignty and mankind's free will work together are a mystery, just like prayer.

A number of years ago I (Jeff) was driving home late at night. I reached a stoplight at an empty intersection. When the light turned green, I started to go but heard a voice say, "Stop!" I stopped and waited. About three seconds later, a truck came barreling through the intersection in the opposite direction. It would have pummeled me if I had driven ahead when the light turned green. Several years later, my whole family was in a head-on collision. There was no voice protecting us then. Why? We don't know. What we do know is who we trust in.

We recently returned from a trip to Disneyland. As we careened through the dark on Space Mountain, we weren't nearly as worried as we should've been. We were speeding around corners, with no idea what was just ahead, and going faster than seemed safe. Yet we had fun because we trusted Disneyland. We trusted that its imagineers had control of the situation and would keep us safe. If we can trust a theme park that much, shouldn't we trust God more when we feel like things are speeding too fast, and we can't see what's coming around the corner?

We all have a tendency to only look at our own little micro view. We have a magnifying glass on our own world and circumstances. God is the only one who is capable of stepping back and seeing the whole picture. He is the only one who truly sees the macro view of things.

You may not have any idea what the Lord is doing in the life of your child. You may not see any evidence that He is doing anything at all. Trust Him. He is attentive to you and your child. He sees a much larger picture than you do.

"Surely the arm of the Lord is not too short to save, nor his ear too dull to hear" (Isaiah 59:1).

Look for God Kisses

We call them "God kisses." Some people call them "God winks." We have noticed in our own lives and the lives of others that God will give His people assurances of His love and attention during hard things. It's as if He is saying, "I'm going to allow something that will cause you pain, but here I am."

We have some close friends named Bob and Tammy. They have several children, but one morning at a men's ministry meeting, Bob was especially burdened for their son James. James was running from God, and at the end of the meeting, the men paired up to pray for each other. Bob was paired with a man named Chris who was a pastor from another church. Bob and Chris prayed together for James.

That night James was in a horrible motorcycle accident in Kentucky and airlifted to Nashville. Bob and Tammy got the news and began making arrangements to get from California to Tennessee as fast as possible. They arrived the following day, and guess who met them at the hospital in Nashville? Chris, the pastor who had prayed with Bob the day before for the young man who was now fighting for his life. Chris happened to have flown into Nashville that day for a conference, and when he heard the news immediately went to the hospital to minister to the family.

Chris thought he was going to a conference, but God had a different assignment for him. God used Chris to give Bob and Tammy a kiss from Him and the assurance that He was still God. He was in control of the situation. He loved them and He loved James. That accident was two years ago. James miraculously survived and gave his life back to the God he had been running from. As he fights the hard battle of recovery and physical therapy, he memorizes Scripture to encourage and motivate him forward.

In 2003 our family was in a head-on collision with a woman who was hitting speeds of 85 mph. Our car flipped and we landed sideways on the side of the road. Our youngest son, Wesley, was unconscious. We were dazed and didn't even know whether Wesley was alive. Our daughter Haley started screaming. We didn't know what to do but thought we smelled gas and realized we needed to get the kids out of the car. Jeff grabbed Wesley and started to head out the back of the car. A man was standing there. He was a paramedic who had just gotten off work and was two cars behind us when the accident happened. He grabbed Wesley and began evaluating him. As soon as we had gotten the other kids out of the car, another man came running up. He was an off-duty fireman who was driving by. These two men worked on our kids until the ambulance and life flight arrived. Thank God, everyone recovered from their injuries, but during the scary nights when we didn't know the extent of Wesley's brain damage, we remembered those two men who God orchestrated to be in just the right place at the right time to take care of our family.

In their book *Hope Heals*, Jay and Katherine Wolf tell the story of Katherine's suffering a catastrophic stroke at the age of twenty-six. Katherine and Jay have had to endure an incredible amount of pain. Prior to the stroke, Katherine attended a baby shower at a Southern California bungalow that had been built in the 1920s. She fell in love with it and told Jay she would love to have a house like that someday. Months later, when she was finally released to go home from the hospital, everything aligned perfectly for the Wolfs to not only buy the very bungalow Katherine had loved but two right next to it as well. One to live in, one to rent, and one for Jay's sister to live in as Katherine's caregiver.

God kisses don't always involve accidents. The last four years have been the hardest years of our lives both personally and in ministry. I (Jeff) have always had a thing for Ford Mustangs. I've had several fixer-uppers through the years but have always had to sell them for various reasons. A few weeks ago, a friend of a friend approached me. He had heard that I loved Mustangs. He was getting ready to move out of state, needed to get rid of his '65, and wanted it to go to someone who would really appreciate it. The car hadn't been driven since the '90s, but it was straight. With a car like that, you never really know the value until you dig into it to see what's wrong and what it's got. He didn't want very much for it and I happened to have the money (from the sale of another Mustang), so I bought it and towed it home. You always hear about the "barn find." Let me tell you, the more we learn about this rare car, the more we realize it was quite the barn find! My wife says we don't have time for me to give you all the specs, but email me and I'll be more than happy to go on and on. That car is a God kiss!

A year and a half ago we were able to move into our dream home. It is literally a house we cannot afford in an area we are easily priced out of. The Lord orchestrated everything so beautifully that our bills are actually cheaper here than at our former home, which was worth considerably less. This home is a God kiss!

A God kiss doesn't have to be dramatic or material either. It is simply recognizing the gracious gifts of a Father who loves you even in the midst of hard things. We are always troubled when people can't find anything to be thankful for. They're just not looking. We have some friends who are suffering tremendously. The hits just keep coming for them, and our hearts break with each new trial they have to go through. They just sold their two-story house because they need a single story. While looking for a new home, one of the things on their list of wants was a nice view.

They looked at several homes in the country with gorgeous views, but the problem is, they are city folk through and through. The thought of trying to manage acreage was overwhelming to them, so they gave up on the view and started looking for something more practical. They fell in love with a home on a nice cul-de-sac in the city and bought it. Each day as they walk out their front door, if they look a certain direction at just the right time, there is a beautiful view. Our friend has pointed out several times that she knows the view is a God kiss.

Read God's Word

Just like Scripture was the road map for Corrie and Betsie ten Boom, Scripture is our answer to most situations we find ourselves in. A few days ago we were deeply wounded by someone. We griped to each other about it. We received encouragement from others who were aware of the situation that the lady who said mean and careless words to us was totally out of order. We rehearsed, in our heads and out loud to each other, over and over again, what we should say back to her. After a couple of hours, it dawned on us that we had done several things but not the one thing that Scripture tells us to do. We stopped, repented, and prayed for the one who had wounded us.

God's Word is full of wisdom. The problem is that it usually doesn't quite jibe with our wisdom. Our preference wasn't to pray for that lady. Our preference was to gather as many people as possible to tell us that we are great and she is terrible and then to let her know how terrible her words were. We've searched and searched, but we can't seem to find the verse in the Bible that tells us to do that. So we prayed for her instead because if we really believe that God is God, then we have to believe that He knows better than we do. We also have to believe that when His Word says it, He means it.

God's Word is chock-full of road map Scriptures to navigate us through difficult or confusing situations like the ones above. God's Word is also full of encouraging examples like the ones we mentioned at the beginning of this chapter. Read their stories and the stories of others who have endured pain with perseverance. And when you read their stories, really pause and think about what their circumstances were like. Paul spent a day and a night in the open sea. Think about that. Peter and the apostles were flogged for preaching in the name of Jesus. Think about how that would have felt. But then they "left the Sanhedrin, rejoicing because they had been counted worthy of suffering disgrace for the Name" (Acts 5:41). These were real people, and if they can persevere, so can we.

Don't Accept Improper Judgment

We sat at a coffee shop with a young lady whose husband is addicted to drugs. She has young children and struggles to hide money from him so she can buy food and diapers. She told us that when she sits in church, she feels like everyone else is so happy and carefree, and she is the only one with a messed-up life. That's the belief, isn't it? We have pastored people for over thirty years. We hear the things that no one else does. We want you to try an exercise this Sunday when you sit in your seat at church. Do a 360 look around the room. We may not pastor your specific church, but we will promise you that as you looked around the room, you saw people living with incredibly painful circumstances— lots of them. It doesn't matter what they looked like on the outside, how impeccably they were dressed, or how much they love the Lord. You laid eyes on many people who have cried themselves to sleep recently. We'd bet the farm on it.

Pain is universal though it is not all the same. We tend to jockey for position and feel good about ourselves if we're not going through as much as the person over there. We can even unconsciously fall into the trap of those in Jesus's day who assumed that if you suffered, you had sinned. They must have forgotten to read the book of Job. Even though the phrase "Don't judge" is overused, the action is underused.

We are absolutely allowed to lovingly correct someone who is in sin. We are also to recognize a tree by its fruit and protect ourselves and others from those who bear bad fruit (Matthew 7:1–5, 15–20). However, we take things too far and sinfully judge when we talk about or correct people without love for them being our motivation, when we turn our assumptions into facts, or when we want to decide the punishment they deserve.

I (Jeff) hate avocados. I live in California, and it's a tough place to be an avocado hater. I joke about it from time to time. A lady in my church approached me on Sunday to let me know that she was extremely offended by my dislike of that squishy green fruit. She also enlightened me that my feelings about avocados stem from my relationship with my father. She is not a therapist and has never met my father. She had turned her assumptions into facts and spoke of things she knew nothing about.

I (Diana) grew up knowing that my paternal grandfather had abandoned my grandma and dad when my dad was two years old. I always thought he was terrible. What kind of man does that? I met him when I was seventeen and he seemed nice enough, but I still held a grudge against him for how he had treated the people I love. Before my grandma died, she told me more about her past.

She had married my grandfather when they were both in their teens. During her pregnancy he was sent off to WWll. She said that when he came home, it was the strangest thing—he went back to live with his parents and acted like they had never been married. He would have barely been in his twenties. My heart went out to him. Knowing what we now know about PTSD and the horrors of WWll, I can understand why a very young man wanted to go back to the safety of another time in his life. He once randomly sent my dad $1,000. He tried to make amends; he just didn't know how. I had judged him without knowing all the facts. I still don't know all the facts. God knows all the facts, and God will judge him correctly.

Maybe you have been treated that way. Maybe others have made assumptions without knowing the facts and labeled you a bad parent. Or maybe there are rumors that there must be something going on in your family, and that is why your kids turned out how they did. Don't allow it. It's true that you can't chase down and correct every rumor. We've tried that, and it's kind of like the whack-a-mole game at the fair. Don't wear yourself out. You can't always defend yourself, but you are the one who gets to decide which words and accusations stick to you.

When something untrue is said about you, it hurts so deeply. Give that situation and person to God, and let their words fall to the ground. Do not take those words in and allow them to germinate in your mind. When something is said about you that is true, repent, change, and give that situation to God. The devil is an accuser. The Holy Spirit convicts to lead us to repentance. They look and sound different. If what you're hearing makes you feel like there is no hope, God could never love you, and you need to give up, those are accusations. They come from the father of lies, and you don't have to allow them to land. It is absolutely true that you were not a perfect parent. It is also true that only God knows all of the facts about your family, and no one else has the right to judge you.

Allow Others to Hold You Up

Yes, some people will judge you. That's unavoidable. There should be people in your sphere, though, who will embody Romans 12:15 and will "rejoice with those who rejoice" and "mourn with those who mourn." Find those people.

The first place to look is your spouse, if you have one. If you are married and both followers of Jesus, you need to be praying together, especially if you have a prodigal child. Sometimes couples feel awkward praying together. Start small. As you pray for your meal, add in a prayer for your child and each other. As you grow more comfortable with that, move your prayer to a time in your day when you can devote more attention to it.

We pray together every morning after we finish our coffee and before we start our day. We like to have around 30–45 minutes, but sometimes we sleep in too long or someone has an early morning meeting. Though we might get cut short or interrupted every once in a while, that's an exception, not the norm. Sometimes we also pray when we go to bed. We always stop what we're doing and pray together when something unexpected happens. We don't do it because we're pious or trying to win God's approval. We do it because we are needy, and we simply don't have the strength to handle life's pains without regularly talking to God together. We are also a bit addicted to peace and joy, which are impossible to maintain with any consistency without dumping our worries and problems on our heavenly Father.

As powerful as praying together as a couple is, you still can't go it alone. You need others to come alongside and pray with you. Turn the page and we'll show you how.

CHAPTER 8

BATTLE CRY: THE NEED FOR COMMUNITY

J ake and Stephanie have been friends of ours for years. They had the type of family everyone else at church was jealous of. They were definitely perfect parents. We met when our kids were in grade school, and it was a match made in heaven. We became great friends, and their kids are some of our kids' closest friends. It was rare not to have a get-together of some sort between our families at least once a month. So it was odd when Jake and Stephanie seemed to pull back from us. There was always a reason they couldn't get together or go out to dinner with us, and it became so frequent that we began to worry we had offended them somehow.

Unbeknownst to us, Jake and Stephanie were having a terrible time with one of their teenage children. They were being crushed under the burden of all the pain and worry they were going through with this child as well as the need to keep the situation a secret. They were the family that everyone else in the church strived to imitate, and for people to know what was going on would be humiliating. They also felt the need to protect their child's reputation.

Fortunately, Jake and Stephanie knew they couldn't continue the way they were going. One day a mutual friend stopped by to borrow something, and the dam broke. Stephanie tearfully poured out her troubled heart to this friend and then asked the question, "Have you got me?" What she meant was, "Will you help me carry this? Can I count on you to still love and respect me? Will you still love my child? Will you not gossip about me?"

A few weeks later, I (Diana) sat at lunch with Stephanie while she poured out everything to me. She had experienced the relief of bringing someone else into the situation and wanted to include a few more trusted couples. We began praying for this child of theirs and that they would have the wisdom to navigate this storm.

A few years later when our own child came to us, struggling with their faith in Christ, Jake and Stephanie were some of the first people we reached out to for support. There was a peace in knowing we wouldn't be judged by them because they had walked this road before. Within a few months, not only did another of Jake and Stephanie's kids begin rebelling but several other friends began struggling with their children. As we are pastors, they would often come to us timid, embarrassed, and not wanting anyone else to know.

One evening we got mad. We knew of so many parents who were struggling with a teenage or adult child, and all of them were islands of isolation, not wanting anyone to know that their family wasn't perfect. As we talked about in chapter 2, that's exactly where the enemy wants us. We decided to do something about it. We contacted each couple individually and asked if they would be willing to get together with a small group to share and pray for our kids.

Battle Cry was born! There were four couples that first night. We shared, cried, prayed, and encouraged one another. As we got ready to go home, Jake observed that, although nothing had changed, he felt as if a weight had been lifted off him. He felt hope and joy. The rest of us agreed that we felt the same.

RESTORE THE ROAD HOME

You need community. We all need community. Scripture warns us in 2 Timothy 3:1–4, "There will be terrible times in the last days. People will be lovers of themselves, lovers of money, boastful, proud, abusive, disobedient to their parents, ungrateful, unholy, without love, unforgiving, slanderous, without self-control, brutal, not lovers of the good, treacherous, rash, conceited, lovers of pleasure rather than lovers of God." Terrible times are coming, and many would argue they are already upon us. This Scripture certainly describes much of what we see in society and even in some of our families.

How are we to navigate such turmoil? As we talked about in the last chapter, Scripture gives us the road map. "Let us hold unswervingly to the hope we profess, for he who promised is faithful. And let us consider how we may **spur one another** on toward love and good deeds, **not giving up meeting together**, as some are in the habit of doing, but **encouraging one another**—and **all the more as you see the Day approaching**" (Hebrews 10:23–25). One thing we know about the pandemic of 2020 is that after lockdowns were lifted, many people did not return to church. If the enemy's only strategy during that pandemic was to get people in the church to feel that watching online is good enough and they don't need to be in regular fellowship with other believers, he did a pretty good job. But God's Word tells us to meet together **more**, not less, as we see the end coming.

I (Jeff) was a pastor for K-LOVE Radio for fifteen years. I took thousands of phone calls from people who professed to be Christians but did not belong to a church. When tragedy hit, they had no one to turn to for prayer, encouragement, and support, so they had to call a stranger at a radio station hundreds of miles away. That is not the way God designed us to live. As Christians, we belong to His family. We need to be in fellowship with His family. Is our family a bit annoying or dysfunctional sometimes? Sure! That's not an excuse to not gather together. If you are not currently attending a church, in person where people know you, find one. You may have to visit a few. You won't find a perfect one. But you need to be in church and meeting together with people who really know you.

Charles Spurgeon said, "If I had never joined a church till I had found one that was perfect, I should never have joined one at all. And the moment I did join it, if I had found one, I should have spoiled it, for it would not have been a perfect church after I had become a member of it. Still, imperfect as it is, it is the dearest place on earth to us."

WHY WE NEED COMMUNITY

There are many reasons God has designed us to live in a community of fellow believers. We want to point out just a few of them.

Encouragement

To encourage someone literally means to infuse them with courage. The troubles we face in this life have a way of sucking the courage right out of us. We all need people to remind us who we are sometimes. We need people to remind us how great our Father is. We need people to remind us that we can be strong when our knees are quaking. We need people who will speak words of courage into us. We need to know that others are lifting our pain up to our heavenly Father. And we need to be doing the same for them.

"And we urge you, brothers and sisters, warn those who are idle and disruptive, encourage the disheartened, help the weak, be patient with everyone" (1 Thessalonians 5:14).

Interesting that as we were finishing up this section, we just received a text from Stephanie that simply said, "Praying for your children!! Xoxo." We are encouraged!

Variety of Gifts

God loves diversity. He created it! We often say that God is not a cookie-cutter God. He has personally fashioned each one of us with different skills, loves, and giftings. Aren't you glad you don't have to be everything but can focus on the piece that God intends for you to fill. For that to happen, others need to be fulfilling their responsibilities to use their giftings too.

Early on at one of our Battle Cry prayer meetings, one of the men in the group had a vision for each child we were praying for. He had never had that happen before, and he just kept saying things like, "OK, I don't understand this, but this is what I'm seeing . . ." After he described what he was seeing with each child, the parent confirmed that what he saw spoke to what that child was going through. Nobody else had a vision that night, but this man operated in that gift and it blessed our whole group. We all benefited, and it gave us better direction as we prayed.

A couple of years ago, I (Diana) received a phone call one morning from a lady in our group. She said she had felt the Lord wake her up at 5:00 that morning with our prodigal child and me on her heart. So she prayed. I thanked her. That's always a good feeling when someone lets you know that you were prayed for. Later that morning our child called to let me know they were separating from their spouse. It was one of the hardest phone calls I have ever received, but I was unusually calm. God already knew the news I was going to receive that day and used this precious lady to give me a God kiss.

> There are different kinds of gifts, but the same Spirit distributes them. There are different kinds of service, but the same Lord. There are different kinds of working, but in all of them and in everyone it is the same God at work. Now to each one the manifestation of the Spirit is given for the common good. To one there is given through the Spirit a message of wisdom, to another a message of knowledge by means of the same

Spirit, to another faith by the same Spirit, to another gifts of healing by that one Spirit, to another miraculous powers, to another prophecy, to another distinguishing between spirits, to another speaking in different kinds of tongues, and to still another the interpretation of tongues. All these are the work of one and the same Spirit, and he distributes them to each one, just as he determines. Just as a body, though one, has many parts, but all its many parts form one body, so it is with Christ. (1 Corinthians 12:4–12)

Rest for the Weary

Sometimes you're just done, and you feel like you can't even pray. At one of our recent prayer meetings, I (Jeff) felt the Lord give me a word for one of the ladies in the group. She and her husband have received hit after hit, and they are weary. As we were all praying, I went up to her and told her to just rest and listen to the worship music. We would do the praying that night. She didn't have to do anything. Her kids would all be lifted before the throne of God, and she could be refreshed in worship. She began to cry as I just hugged her. She was too weary to even pray that night, but we had her back.

During the brutal trench warfare of WWI, individual soldiers actually spent little time in the trenches. The battle was so hard that infantrymen would be sent to fight for one to six days on average. Then they would be withdrawn from the front lines to perform other tasks. A typical British soldier's time was divided with about 15 percent on the front line and 20 percent resting. The majority of their time was used on the support line, working in the infirmary, etc.

It doesn't matter how strong you are—you will need relief from the front line. You need an army around you to take your place and battle while you are resting. You need people in the spiritual hospital to dress your emotional wounds, so you can go back out and engage your enemy.

What a relief it is to know that we can take some rest time, but the enemy is still feeling the sting of warriors' prayers for our children.

"Carry each other's burdens, and in this way you will fulfill the law of Christ. . . . Let us not become weary in doing good, for at the proper time we will reap a harvest if we do not give up. Therefore, as we have opportunity, let us do good to all people, especially to those who belong to the family of believers" (Galatians 6:2, 9–10).

Emergency Support

I (Diana) was hanging up lights in our backyard this weekend. I almost walked out the back door without my phone but then thought better of it. I would be up on a tall ladder, reaching to get lights in the places I wanted them. If I fell, I would need to be able to get a hold of someone quickly.

Sometimes we fall. We may fall physically, but we also fall emotionally and spiritually. We need our people who we can call at any hour when a crisis hits. We have a text thread for our group, so we can communicate any updates or prayer needs that arise. We have also all given permission to be contacted in the middle of the night, if need be, when someone needs immediate prayer or comfort. This privilege has never been abused, and it's such a good feeling to know there are people who will be there for you at any hour.

"Be devoted to one another in love. Honor one another above yourselves. Never be lacking in zeal, but keep your spiritual fervor, serving the Lord. Be joyful in hope, patient in affliction, faithful in prayer. Share with the Lord's people who are in need. Practice hospitality. . . . Rejoice with those who rejoice; mourn with those who mourn" (Romans 12:10–13, 15).

HOW TO START A GROUP

Maybe you're on board with the need for a group of brothers and sisters in Christ to support, encourage, and pray for you. Where do you start?

Friends

The first group we started happened organically because several couples in our friend group were struggling with one or more of their children. That's a great place to start! Hopefully you have some friends who you can be authentic and vulnerable with, and they can be the same with you. If that's the case, then it simply takes asking if they would be willing to get together to pray for your kids. In our first Battle Cry group, we even had a couple who wasn't having any problems with their kids. They just loved the rest of us and wanted to pray for us too.

Life Groups

Does your church have Life Groups, small groups, or any other kind of "meet in the home" groups? Talk with your church leaders about making one of them a Battle Cry group to pray for prodigal children. The group we have now is a Life Group at our church. It still contains two of the original members of the first one, but we opened it up to more people.

Church

If you have a heart for starting a Battle Cry prayer group but your church doesn't already have a small group model for you to follow, talk to your church leaders about throwing the idea out to the congregation to gauge interest. You don't need many. Three to five couples is a good size (more on this later in the pitfalls section).

Community

Bringing up the idea of a community Battle Cry group is more a caution than a suggestion. In our experience, it's better to stick with people you know. You will all be discussing very personal and delicate things. You need to trust the people you are sharing with. You also need to make sure that you share the same theology on essential matters. That being said, a Battle Cry group open to the community, provided it had some mature leaders, could be a great outreach to families who are hurting and don't know where to turn.

HOW TO RUN A GROUP

As we have already mentioned, God loves diversity! Jeff loves to pray loud with music blasting. Diana prefers it much quieter. We don't want to micromanage how you run your meetings, but we do want to share some of the ways we have done it as well as some mistakes we've made along the way.

The first step is finding a regular time that works for everyone. We have met once a week and every other week. Do what is going to be best for your group without burning anyone out. We make sure we have drinks and dessert or some finger foods set out, and we're good to go.

First Meeting

When we start a new group, we set aside the first meeting to tell our stories. Let everyone know beforehand, and plan to spend the whole evening sharing. This is surprisingly therapeutic because we often keep our pain bottled up, and it is a relief to get it all out. Be sure to have tissues available.

The first meeting is also the time to exchange phone numbers, set up a text thread, and go over rules. There are not many, but they are important.

Rules

1. Everything talked about in our group is confidential.

This should go without saying but still needs to be said. Your group is a vault, and nothing is repeated. The one exception is in cases of abuse. If you are leading a group and you strongly suspect or know that a child is being abused, you need to contact the proper authorities.

2. Never approach someone's child and tell them you are praying for them.

This happened in one of our groups. It was well meant, of course. But it caused this child to feel like his parents were talking about him to others and broke down some trust in the relationship.

3. There is no judgment.

You are going to hear ugly things, and you're going to be shocked. This is the rule that the couples in our group tend to find the most comfort in. Be prepared to hear about mental illness, suicidal thoughts, sexual addictions, sexual confusion, violence, and a variety of crimes. We always tell our group that we will not judge them and we will not judge their children no matter what they tell us. We will fall to our knees and pray.

4. This is a time to pray, not give unsolicited parenting advice.

We're not saying that suggestions or helpful observations can't ever be made, but discernment must be used. Nobody is here for a counseling session. We are here to pray. Sometimes someone will need advice, and it is totally appropriate to spend time there as there is "wisdom in a multitude of counsel." However, taking time away from prayer to share wisdom with someone in the group shouldn't be a regular thing that monopolizes the meetings.

5. Commitment is vital.

It takes time to build trust, vulnerability, and honesty among people. When someone misses the meetings often, they will not be as close to the rest of the group. They will also miss important updates from each family that will have to be repeated or overlooked. Obviously, things come up and sometimes someone won't be able to make it. There is always grace when that happens, but making a commitment to prioritize the group meetings is important.

MEETING STRUCTURE

The way you run your weekly or biweekly meetings is largely up to you. We always start with any updates. Sometimes there are none and we jump right into prayer. Sometimes there are a lot or one family is having a particularly hard week, and we spend more time bringing encouragement or praying for a specific family or child. Let the Holy Spirit lead you. As long as you are spending time praying for and encouraging one another, you have succeeded! We actually change it up from meeting to meeting. We do different styles of praying so we don't get in a rut. Here are a few of the ways we have conducted our prayer time.

1. Popcorn Prayer

Jeff usually opens in prayer, and then we leave it open for anyone to pray as they feel led. Once every child has been prayed for and the prayers seem to be winding down, Jeff will have someone close in prayer.

2. Yell Out Prayer

We didn't really know what to call this one, so "yell out prayer" it is. We put on some worship music. Everyone goes to a place in the house where they feel comfortable. Someone is in charge of yelling out a child's or family's name every five minutes. We all pray at the same time for that child/family until the next name is yelled out. When every child or family has been prayed for, we come together and someone closes in prayer.

3. Couple in the Middle

Each couple takes turns being surrounded by the whole group. One to three designated people will pray for the couple and their children. Then we move on to the next couple.

You can also separate the men and women to pray together, pair up couples, etc. It really is simple. The important thing is that you are praying for these weary families and wandering children. How you do it is entirely up to you. Feel free to get creative and ask what the people in your group like best. Our group tends to do "yell out prayer" the most.

Pitfalls

There are seriously no words to describe what a blessing our Battle Cry groups have been to us and others. That doesn't mean there haven't been some lessons learned and things we should have done differently.

When we started our first group, we were so delighted to see heartbroken parents being encouraged. We wanted everyone to feel that way! Whenever a couple came to us with a burden for one of their children, we would invite them to our group.

When we first started meeting, we would sometimes spend two hours in prayer. With each new couple, that time grew. We tried different ways to be more time efficient, like splitting up men and women, but the group was just too big to be effective. Even the most valiant prayer warriors have to go home and get to bed at some point. We try to keep our current meetings around an hour and a half.

Another problem was that whenever a new person joined, everyone had to retell their stories. This was time-consuming and sometimes painful. It also meant that those of us who had been there since the beginning were hearing the same stories over and over again.

For these reasons, we revamped the group and capped it at three to five family groups (couples or a single parent). We take one night to share all the painful details and then everyone is in the know. After that we do quick updates and get right to prayer.

Because we don't want anyone who is hurting turned away, we have one couple in our group that is on standby to split off and start another group when we have at least two more families who want to join.

Another pitfall we recently discovered was that a somber mood had settled on our meetings. We talk about and pray for serious stuff. There are usually tears. A few weeks ago we just naturally started talking, chatting, and laughing together as good friends should. We decided that we would spend the entire evening that way. We ate and shared fun stories and thoroughly enjoyed one another. We had forgotten to have fun together, and that night was like a breath of fresh air for us. Don't allow the pain you are all going through to steal your joy. It's OK and even necessary at times to take a night to simply be friends and have fun.

As much as we would love to take credit for coming up with the idea to gather parents of prodigals to pray together, that seed was planted by God in me (Jeff) years ago. One of the classes I took in Bible college was called Radical Discipleship. It was the '80s and that was an awesome name for a class. Our professor encouraged us to look for opportunities to have encounters with people, so we could share the love of Christ with them.

Late one night I was at a gas station in Sacramento with a classmate. I saw a young man walking back and forth near the dumpster. He looked upset, and I felt the Holy Spirit tell me to go check on him. I thought that was kind of crazy, so I mentioned it to my friend. He simply said, "You'd better do it."

I hesitantly approached the man, who looked like he was high, and asked him if he was OK. He turned to me and said, "I was just asking God, if He was real, to send someone to help me." Turns out this young man had run away from home and gotten involved in drugs. All he wanted was to get back home to his parents.

His parents lived in a town in the foothills of the Sierra Nevadas. It was a bit of a drive and it was now well after midnight, but we agreed to take him home. As we shared Christ with him, he sobered up immediately, repented, and surrendered his life to the lordship of Jesus.

When we arrived at his parents' house, he insisted that we come in to meet them. We felt a bit awkward about that since it was so late, but as we got out of the truck, we heard the sound of beautiful music. We walked into a house filled with worship music and several people praying for this young man. We had the honor of interrupting their meeting to deliver this prodigal son back to his parents.

I have never seen that family again, but what I saw the Lord do that night was one of the most impactful events of my life. It doesn't matter what your child has done or where they have walked. Our God leaves the ninety-nine to go after the one. He redeems and restores. He is mighty to save! If you are a parent going through the pain of having a wandering child, take heart. Gather an army who will link arms with you and battle your mutual enemy. We will win, but we can't do it alone.

"Surely the arm of the Lord is not too short to save, nor his ear too dull to hear" (Isaiah 59:1).

CHAPTER 9

DON'T BURN THE BRIDGE

O ur three children are an absolute blessing from God. Regard-
less of where their walk with the Lord stands or whatever
hard conversations we've had with them at different times,
they are gifts from God Himself, and they are pretty spectacular ones!

"Children are a heritage from the Lord, offspring a reward from
him. . . . Blessed is the man whose quiver is full of them" (Psalm
127:3, 5).

We hope you'll allow us a moment to gush about our kids. Jordan,
our oldest son, is brilliant. He loves learning and he's one of those
deep thinkers. Conversations with him are never boring. He thinks up
solutions to societal problems in his head and jokes about writing his
manifesto someday. He feels deeply and has a desire to champion those
who are marginalized. He's also funny and can do multiple accents and
character voices.

Our only daughter, Haley, is sweet, thoughtful, and charming. She can
tend to be the life of the party, but we've always been impressed with
how she uses her popularity to include and build up rather than exclude
and degrade others. She is kind and often stresses about making sure
she is treating people well. She loves to dance and is a very talented
performer.

DON'T BURN THE BRIDGE

Wesley is the baby of the family, and he is calm, quiet, and kind. He never has a harsh or negative word to say about anybody. Seriously, we honestly think he sees nothing but the best in people. He is faithful and a man of his word. If you are fortunate enough to be his friend he will stick by you forever, no matter what. Wesley loves tech stuff and all kinds of gadgets. Lighting is his specialty.

It's true that our kids have faults too. But we wanted to begin this chapter focusing on the beautiful people that God has created them to be because sometimes, especially if you have a child not serving the Lord, there can be the tendency to fixate on what you want to change in them and forget to view them as the delightful gifts from God that they are. Yes, we want our children to return to a thriving relationship with God. But in the meantime, they are still our children. In this chapter we want to talk about how to maintain a healthy, loving relationship with our kids no matter where they are in their spiritual journey.

A few years ago a lady asked us to do premarital counseling with her daughter and her daughter's fiancé. She was very clear that we could not meet with them in her home. Curious, we asked why. She told us that her future son-in-law was not allowed in her home because he was not a Christian. Friends, our Master ate with sinners.

> As he walked along, he saw Levi son of Alphaeus sitting at the tax collector's booth. "Follow me," Jesus told him, and Levi got up and followed him. While Jesus was having dinner at Levi's house, many tax collectors and sinners were eating with him and his disciples, for there were many who followed him. When the teachers of the law who were Pharisees saw him eating with the sinners and tax collectors, they asked his disciples: "Why does he eat with tax collectors and sinners?" On hearing this, Jesus said to them, "It is not the healthy who need a doctor, but the sick. I have not come to call the righteous, but sinners." (Mark 2:14–17)

If you believe that you can't spend time with your kids because of their lifestyle, then you need to take a fresh look at who Jesus spent time with. Yes, it's true that Jesus's goal was to bring healing and freedom to those who were bound by sin. But it's also true that He didn't sit there eating dinner with them grudgingly. He enjoyed them because He loved them. That's why the Pharisees were so put out.

LOVE

The first step to maintaining a good relationship with your child is to love and enjoy them even if you don't agree with them or their choices. The starting point of everything we do should be love—love for God and love for others.

> Hearing that Jesus had silenced the Sadducees, the Pharisees got together. One of them, an expert in the law, tested him with this question: "Teacher, which is the greatest commandment in the Law?" Jesus replied: "'Love the Lord your God with all your heart and with all your soul and with all your mind.' This is the first and greatest commandment. And the second is like it: 'Love your neighbor as yourself.' All the Law and Prophets hang on these two commandments." (Matthew 22:34–40)

Jesus didn't tell us to only love our neighbor if they were following Him and living by a particular moral code.

> If I speak in the tongues of men or of angels, but do not have love, I am only a resounding gong or a clanging cymbal. If I have the gift of prophecy and can fathom all mysteries and all knowledge, and if I have a faith that can move mountains, but do not have love, I am nothing. If I give all I possess to the poor and give

over my body to hardship that I may boast, but do not have love, I gain nothing. Love is patient, love is kind. It does not envy, it does not boast, it is not proud. It does not dishonor others, it is not self-seeking, it is not easily angered, it keeps no record of wrongs. Love does not delight in evil but rejoices with the truth. It always protects, always trusts, always hopes, always perseveres. Love never fails. (1 Corinthians 13:1–8)

This is not to say that you should never point out sin. It is right and loving for your children to know where you stand on issues that will cause them to be bound by sin and its horrible consequences. It is also true that you are not the Holy Spirit, and it's not your job to make them stop sinning. It's your job to love them. That means you warn them when you see them going down a dangerous road, and you give them all the love and support you can even when they keep heading in that direction. That means having hard conversations about what the Bible says about sin but not rejecting them for their sin.

When our hearts are starting at a place of love, we will speak truth because we love our child too much to see them make harmful choices without warning them. But we will also love big because we know that we are not better or superior; we have simply been cleansed by the only one who has lived without sin and the only one who can judge our child.

It's easy to get so gung-ho to fight with our child over issues that we forget to love. Your child is not your enemy. Your child is a gift from the Lord. Sometimes we get so upset that anger and resentment can well up inside us toward our own precious offspring. Or we're so determined to "fix" them and win the debate that we forget to listen. In your exuberance to win your child back to the Lord, you can cause more damage if your motivation is anything other than love, so let's talk about how and when to engage without burning down that bridge.

We used to live in a one-hundred-year-old home. We loved it! It had all the charm you would expect. We had a dry rot issue though. The south side of our house started showing a little bit of damage. We were able to ignore it for a while. It didn't look too bad. Honestly, if we would have just slapped some paint on it, we could have camouflaged the ugliness and kept on living with it.

Wisdom doesn't gloss over damage with a fresh coat of paint. Unfortunately, the wisest course usually creates a huge mess and costs a great deal. Since we don't like mess and expense, we often avoid it until it can't be ignored any longer. Our cute century-old home finally got to the point that we could poke a finger right through the siding. It was time to really see the damage. We peeled back the siding to find that the rot had infected the studs and even part of the foundation. It was only after this that we could employ more active tools to repair the damage.

TOOLS TO REPAIR YOUR RELATIONSHIP

Listen

Listening to your child helps you peel back the external and see what's underneath. It seems too passive to be helpful, but it is the vital first step to progress. We will warn you that what you hear may be true, it may be false, or it may be a mixture of both. It will almost certainly be upsetting and uncomfortable at times. Kind of like ripping the siding off your house, it will make you feel vulnerable and exposed. So how do you deal with what you hear as you allow your child the privilege of being heard?

First, you have to come to terms with the fact that you didn't do everything right. We've joked several times about being perfect parents. We know that we're not, and that knowledge is incredibly painful. Parenting is the job we want to excel at most in the world, and at times we have failed. Even the best parents make mistakes.

Repent

When your child brings up things that are true, you need to repent. We know that hurts and it's hard, but this is our first active tool. You need to repent before God and ask your child to forgive you. If you feel like you can't apologize and ask your child to forgive you, because you're the parent, you need to get over yourself. Repentance and forgiveness are integral parts of the Christian life. To imagine you would never have to apologize to one of the people closest to you is a farce. We have both had to apologize multiple times to all of our children throughout the years. Make it a lifestyle and it won't be excruciating, although it may always be hard.

Clarify

Perhaps the hardest part of listening is hearing things that have been misconstrued or are flat-out wrong. Now is not the time to stop listening. Pause, breathe, pray a quick prayer, and then bring clarification. Ask more questions if you need to, but continue to treat them in a loving way. If your child believes an untruth, you will not convince them otherwise by interrupting, yelling, or reacting in anger.

Once your child has aired their grievances, and you've asked for forgiveness for anything you have done wrong, now is the time to bring your perspective to things they may not be seeing clearly. You are allowed to defend yourself, and you are allowed to be human. You need to give grace and mercy to your child, but let them know that you expect the same in return. I read a post recently that stated, "The job of parents is to do the best they can at the moment, with God's help, and the job of children is to forgive their parents' mistakes, with God's help." Maybe our adult children don't realize that their parents need grace too. It's OK to let them know that.

We hurt one of our kids a couple of years ago. We were going through a very emotionally painful time. We were having a big event, and extending an invitation to someone who was very dear to this child would have exacerbated the pain we were going through. It really wasn't even the fault of the person we weren't going to invite. They had done nothing wrong. But them being there would have highlighted our sorrow that someone else who should have been there wasn't. We asked for prayer about it in our Battle Cry group, and afterward, one of our precious friends gently brought correction to us. We were wrong and acting in a selfish way. We repented, apologized to our child, and fortunately had enough time to extend the invitation that we should have given in the first place. We did our part, even though we had messed up. Then it was our child's job to forgive and not hold that against us. Here are some rules to help you through some of those hard conversations.

RULES FOR HARD CONVERSATIONS

1. Use "I" statements

Focus on how you feel instead of pointing fingers at someone else.

2. Validate Feelings

You don't have to agree in order to validate that you believe someone genuinely feels a certain way.

3. Make Restoration the Goal

You may never come to agreement about something. Restore the relationship anyway. If you have to agree, you may never succeed, but you can always succeed if you make the relationship with each other the most important goal.

As you walk this road, you have to continually rely on the leading of the Holy Spirit. Going back to the picture of our former house, we had to have a professional guide us in the repairs. We didn't always know what to look for or what could cause greater damage down the road. We had to listen to someone else in order to discover the extent of the damage in places we couldn't see. You don't have to go this alone. You have one who loves your child more than you do who will guide you as you seek to love your child well.

4. Rebuild

As we discovered places of damage in our house, we had to remove what was rotten and replace it with new, stronger materials. You may have a relationship with one or more of your children that must be rebuilt because there has been extensive damage. Rebuilding is worth it, but it takes time, intention, and patience.

Imagine that you and your child are on the opposite sides of a bridge with missing or decaying planks. There may have been actions that aggressively ripped out the planks, or maybe there has been neglect and the planks have rotted, like the side of our house. The goal of rebuilding trust in a relationship is that both of you can safely walk across the bridge to each other. For that to happen, new planks need to be laid down, and there must be courage to walk across.

If you have been responsible for removing some of the planks, you need to make an effort to replace them. You may need to replace three or four planks before your child will feel comfortable putting one foot on the bridge. Be patient and ask your child to acknowledge that you've put a board down, but don't expect them to walk across the whole bridge immediately.

For example, if you have been too busy working to show up to your child's events, you need to ask for forgiveness and start rebuilding the bridge by showing up. If you have had a history of speaking degrading words to your child, you need to apologize and make a practice of speaking only what will build up. But don't expect them to trust the change in you right away. It takes many planks to make a bridge safe enough to walk across. Give them time to learn to trust you.

5. Protect

Our grandson Sebastian is three years old. It seems as if his parents' full-time job is to protect him. Even under their watchful eyes, he still gets bumps, scrapes, and bruises. Protection is one of the first jobs we were given when our children were born, and we are not excused from that job when they become adults.

No, you don't have to hold their hand to cross the street anymore or keep them from running with sharp objects. Now your protection looks different. It means protecting their value, reputation, and dignity.

In John 8:1–11 we read the famous story of the woman caught in adultery. Can you imagine how scared and embarrassed she was, surrounded by men who were using her to trap Jesus and ready to stone her to death? The first thing Jesus did was take the attention off her. He knelt down and began to write in the sand. We don't know exactly what He wrote, but we do know that everyone was now focused on that instead of the woman. Jesus shielded her by his actions. Then, saying His famous words, "Let any one of you who is without sin be the first to throw a stone at her," He protected her and restored her dignity.

As we lovingly ask our children to "sin no more," we still have the job of protecting them. No matter what Jordan does, we are team Jordan. Whatever Haley's life looks like, we are team Haley. Any struggles Wesley goes through, we are team Wesley. We will defend them and speak well of them. We will not allow anyone to harm them in word or deed.

One of the women in our Battle Cry group is very clear that she will only tell us enough about what's going on with her children so that we know how to pray. She purposely leaves things out, even with us, to protect her children's reputations. You should never gossip about or run down your children or allow others to do so.

6. Sacrifice

Listening to the Holy Spirit and obeying His leading often brings us to places of sacrifice. This can take many forms, but love will always be willing to lay down its own desires for another.

I (Diana) attended divorce court with one of our children. I was heartbroken over the divorce, and it took all of my strength not to start sobbing when I saw their names on the docket. But as long as I have any strength in me, my child will not walk through that painful place alone.

As we came through 2020 and all of the conflicts that year induced, one of our friends had an adult child insisting on certain stipulations in order to come home for Christmas. Our friends felt the requirements were too demanding and were about to refuse when the Holy Spirit spoke to them with a question: "Whose house is this? If it's your house, then you get to make the rules." The point was clear to them. This was a home they had dedicated to God. They were not the owners of their stuff—God was. As followers of Christ, we lay down our lives for others. Our friends complied with their child's requests, loved them well, and glorified God.

One note about abuse before we move on. Just as a parent can be abusive to their child, a teen or adult child can be abusive to their parent. We are not telling you to put yourself in danger from someone who is unsafe, even if that person is one you have raised. Yes, you need to be willing to sacrifice for your child, but you should never allow abuse in any form: physical, mental, financial, etc. If your child or the people they are around are too toxic to be in contact with, you may need to love them from afar for right now.

Get creative with what that looks like, but make the effort. That might mean advocating for them to get the mental health services they need. It may look like Christmas and birthday gifts sent through the mail. Our friend Emily is unable to have contact right now with her son because his father, who has full custody in another state, cruelly won't allow her in his life. She buys a birthday card for him every year. Since the father won't allow her to send it to her son, she sends it to herself. She is believing that she will have a relationship with her son again someday and will be able to show him that she remembered every birthday with a postmarked birthday card. She also keeps a journal for him. Even if the circumstances are difficult, make the effort to keep the channels of love open.

7. Let Go

We recommended the book *The Blessing* in an earlier chapter. One of the elements of the blessing that the authors describe is "picturing a special future" for your children. That is such a vital part of raising kids. It comes out in your speech and expectations and communicates value to your sweet offspring. But what happens when the special future we imagined crumbles? What do we do when our child is going in the opposite direction of the glorious life we imagined? We have to let our adult children live their lives without trying to force them to comply with our hopes and dreams.

This can be difficult because there are different seasons of parenting, and you must know which season you are in. The bulk of what babies receive is nurturing. Later discipline is added. Eventually you become your child's coach, and ultimately (hopefully) you are friends. It's a mistake to try to be friends in the discipline season. It's also a mistake to try to discipline when you should simply be coaching. Your child's age determines the season of parenting you are in.

We have to let our adult children make their own choices without taking on any guilt for those choices. Each person on the planet is unique and will have a different journey. Attempting to force your child onto a path that looks like yours will not bear any good fruit and could result in resentment.

In Luke 15, when Jesus told the parables of the lost sheep, lost coin, and lost son, the circumstances and strategies were different with each. The sheep ignorantly wandered away and had to be actively searched for. The coin was lost through carelessness and was also diligently sought after. The son walked away because of willful rebellion and a desire to live a different life. In that instance the father watched and waited.

There may be times when you have to bring clarity to confusion, bring healing to pain, or simply wait for a child to see the world for what it really is. If you are motivated by love and led by the Holy Spirit, you will have all the tools you need for each child in every situation.

CHAPTER 10

FAMILY RELATIONSHIPS

We would be remiss if we didn't acknowledge that having a child walk away from the faith your family embraces can often cause stress points in other family relationships. We want to take a moment to talk about those, so you are not caught by surprise. Some of these areas haven't been a struggle for us, but we have seen these dynamics play out in our friends' lives.

Families, like all of society, are made up of unique and diverse individuals. As we've already talked about, God designed it that way. Our God loves variety, and He doesn't use a cookie cutter when He creates us. Those differences can make us stronger as we all use our gifts for the common good, to build each other up. They can also cause friction and irritation.

We would encourage you to be a student of those differences. Learn what makes your spouse and kids tick. There are many great strength and personality assessments out there. While these can be misused, we believe they are helpful tools to open our eyes to the variety of ways we all think, process, and recharge.

I (Diana) have always been puzzled by Jeff's desire to talk to **everybody**. I've tried to tell him things like, "You can't walk behind the counter at a restaurant to ask the cook how he barbecued his meat." But he does it anyway and usually makes a friend. When he worked at K-LOVE Radio, he was able to take the DISC assessment test. As I read the description of his personality type, my jaw dropped at the accuracy of it. I had to laugh when I read the statement, "Strangers are just friends you haven't met yet." That's my husband.

I (Jeff) have had to learn that my wife is an introvert and what that means. Once, when our children were younger, I asked her what she wanted for her birthday. She wanted alone time at home. I took the kids to her parents' house for the day while she stayed home and read a book. Later she joined us for her birthday dinner, completely happy and recharged. I could have taken offense that she didn't want to be with us all day. But she is always with us, and spending the day alone allowed her to enjoy us even more.

In our family we have a variety of love languages, including touch, time and attention, and words of affirmation. It's important to know that the way we give love might not be the best way our spouse or child receives love and vice versa. The more we understand and affirm the different ways we are made, the more we can love one another well and even stop some conflicts before they start, because we are believing the best about the other person.

This doesn't mean that we allow bad or unhealthy behavior because "that's just how they're made." Our friend Chris Sonksen says something that has been so helpful in striking the balance between acknowledging and accepting our personality bents but not using them as a crutch to avoid change and growth: "Any strength, taken to extreme, becomes a weakness."

We are both pretty active and we love projects. We tend to get bored if we're not fixing something up. As a result, we accomplish a lot. We are big DIYers, and we don't like to procrastinate. That's a strength that has served us well. It has also come around to bite us when we don't keep it under control. We have cut corners on projects because we were too anxious to get it done. We have taken on too much at times and become overwhelmed. A few years ago we restored a vintage trailer. It was difficult but so rewarding in the end. When we saw another one that needed work for sale super cheap, we grabbed it. A few months later, we saw yet another one for free on the side of the road. How could we pass that up? Then we moved to a house that needed fixing up. Now we're overwhelmed, but we still scour the internet for cheap vintage trailers. We need to get that under control.

It's important to understand that our personality types, love languages, ways of processing information, etc. all make up who we are, who our spouse is, and who our children are. Being a student of these things in the people we love helps us empathize with them, enjoy their uniqueness, and gently warn them when their strengths are going to an extreme.

What does all of this have to do with having a prodigal child? A lot, actually. Our personality types cause us to react to hurt, rejection, stress, and conflict differently. For example, if your spouse longs to keep the peace at any cost, they may tend to avoid hard subjects. If you need to talk everything out immediately, you may cause stress to someone who needs to process the problem internally for a little while before talking about it.

Jesus told us, "Blessed are the peacemakers, for they will be called children of God" (Matthew 5:9).

So let's focus on the two areas where it will be most important to work for and encourage peace.

MARRIAGE

Having a child reject the faith in Christ that you hold dear can result in a lot of blame and finger-pointing, even if it's only within your own heart. You may be tempted to replay over and over in your head things your spouse has done wrong or should have done differently. Be on your guard, so you do not become bitter or resentful toward your spouse.

"Make every effort to live in peace with everyone and to be holy; without holiness no one will see the Lord. See to it that no one falls short of the grace of God and that no bitter root grows up to cause trouble and defile many" (Hebrews 12:14–15).

There may be things you need to talk about, repent of, and forgive. The steps we outlined in the last chapter may also need to be used between the two of you if there has been any kind of division or conflict between a parent and child. Colossians 3:21 tells us not to exasperate our children. If your actions have caused bitterness in your child, you may need to rebuild that bridge not only with your child but with your spouse as well.

As we also mentioned in the last chapter, we are designed to be protective of our children. That instinct doesn't change, even if the person we feel we need to protect them from is our spouse. We are not talking about abuse here. If there has been abuse, there needs to be a deeper level of help, counseling, and possibly criminal charges. We are talking about personality clashes. Sometimes a child may either be so similar to a parent or so opposite from a parent that it results in that parent–child relationship having more conflict than others.

If this has happened in your home, you may be tempted to think that your spouse has driven your child away. That may or may not be true. What is true is that you need to make sure you are protecting your marriage from the attacks of the enemy as well as bitterness from each other. If you need professional help, get it. There is no shame in having a therapist navigate you through a tough situation.

If you are in a blended family and one of you is a stepparent, this can become even trickier. A few suggestions if that is the case:

If you are the stepparent, let the biological parent lead.

When it comes to discipline, correction, warning, etc., the biological parent needs to be the main mouthpiece, and the stepparent is the support.

If you are the biological parent, do not allow your child to disrespect your spouse.

You need to stop disrespectful attitudes or speech immediately. If your spouse has sinned or treated your child unfairly, talk to them privately about asking your child for forgiveness.

As the biological parent, it is your job to make sure your spouse and child have the support they need from you to live in harmony with each other. For an excellent resource on blended families, check out *The Smart Stepfamily* by Ron Deal.

Never criticize your spouse to your child (whether you're a blended family or not).

The most important thing, whether you are in a stepparent situation or not, is to remember that you and your spouse are a team. We had some friends who, whenever they got in an argument, would sit side by side on the sofa instead of across from each other. They did this as a visual reminder that they were not opposed to each other but were on the same team, working for the same goals.

SIBLINGS

Siblings have been fighting literally from the beginning. It can be hard enough to keep peace between brothers and sisters without having one reject what the rest of the family believes in. We saw how the older brother didn't make any effort to keep the prodigal from leaving home and then resented him when he returned.

The situation between siblings can be so vastly different, and issues between stepsiblings come into play here too. If your first priority is making peace with your spouse, your second priority is maintaining peace between siblings. With that goal in mind, we have a few suggestions.

Be careful what you share about your child with their siblings.

This doesn't mean you can't share. But before you do, you need to be honest with yourself about why you are sharing. If your goal is to garner prayer and support for your child or to protect their sibling, then evaluate how much needs to be disclosed.

Never pit siblings against one another.

If one of your children has hurt you, you have to be especially careful that you don't attempt to draw sides and get your other children on yours. You need to be using your words to keep the siblings' relationships strong. If you need counsel or a friend to talk to, do that at your Battle Cry group.

Attempt to reconcile siblings who have been hurt by one another.

Sin always harms. You may have children who are angry at one another for the way they have been treated or the way they have seen you treated. Encourage grace. Go back to the example of the father in the parable of the prodigal. The father earnestly tried to get the older son to forgive the younger.

If need be, protect your other children from a harmful sibling.

This is hard because we never want to break up relationships. If you have a child who is toxic, you need to be honest with their siblings and give them proper warning so they are protected. This takes wisdom, and we are not throwing around the word "toxic" lightly. We are talking about situations that would involve verbal, emotional, spiritual, physical, or sexual abuse.

Before we move on, we want to address one more scenario. You may be in a situation where all of your children have banded together and are critical of you. If that is the case, take that hurt to the Lord. He knows what it is like to have everyone He has loved well reject Him. Ask Him to hold your heart, lead you in wisdom, reveal areas where you may need to repent, and help you to continue to love. He will do it. Psalm 55 is a good psalm to meditate on. King David was betrayed by his own son, who turned David's friends against him. David poured out his heart in Psalm 55.

Listen to my prayer, O God,
do not ignore my plea;
hear me and answer me.
My thoughts trouble me and I am distraught
because of what my enemy is saying,
because of the threats of the wicked;
for they bring down suffering on me
and assail me in their anger.

My heart is in anguish within me;
the terrors of death have fallen on me.
Fear and trembling have beset me;
horror has overwhelmed me.
I said, "Oh, that I had the wings of a dove!
I would fly away and be at rest.
I would flee far away
and stay in the desert;
I would hurry to my place of shelter,
far from the tempest and storm."

Lord, confuse the wicked, confound their words,
for I see violence and strife in the city.
Day and night they prowl about on its walls;
malice and abuse are within it.
Destructive forces are at work in the city;
threats and lies never leave its streets.

If an enemy were insulting me,
I could endure it;

if a foe were rising against me,
I could hide.
But it is you, a man like myself,
my companion, my close friend,
with whom I once enjoyed sweet fellowship
at the house of God,
as we walked about
among the worshipers.

Let death take my enemies by surprise;
let them go down alive to the realm of the dead,
for evil finds lodging among them.

As for me, I call to God,
and the Lord saves me.
Evening, morning and noon
I cry out in distress,
and he hears my voice.
He rescues me unharmed
from the battle waged against me,
even though many oppose me.
God, who is enthroned from of old,
who does not change—
he will hear them and humble them,
because they have no fear of God.

My companion attacks his friends;
he violates his covenant.
His talk is smooth as butter,
yet war is in his heart;
his words are more soothing than oil,
yet they are drawn swords.

Cast your cares on the Lord
and he will sustain you;
he will never let

the righteous be shaken.
But you, God, will bring down the wicked
into the pit of decay;
the bloodthirsty and deceitful
will not live out half their days.

But as for me, I trust in you.

You will not walk this road perfectly. We have not walked it perfectly. That is why we are so thankful for grace. When you mess up, let our heavenly Father pour buckets of grace on you, and then get up and start afresh.

"I remember my affliction and my wandering, the bitterness and the gall. I well remember them, and my soul is downcast within me. Yet this I call to mind and therefore I have hope: Because of the Lord's great love we are not consumed, for his compassions never fail. They are new every morning; great is your faithfulness" (Lamentations 3:19–23).

CHAPTER 11

A MESSAGE FOR
THE PRODIGAL

If you have stumbled upon this book and you are one who is currently wandering away from the faith you grew up in, can we talk for just a moment? Please don't be offended if you saw this book on your parent's nightstand or in their bookshelf. The fact that they are reading it is evidence of their love for you.

If your parents are Christians, they believe, with their whole hearts, that God is so full of love that He wanted children to lavishly pour out His love upon. So He created mankind. But love isn't love if it controls others or insists on its own way. Because of that, God gave humans the gift of a free will. Like any good parent, He instructs and warns His kids about things He is aware of that we may not be. We can choose to trust Him and listen, or we can choose to reject Him and follow our own path. The crazy part is, we have all chosen the latter. That doesn't mean we are all currently choosing to reject Him, but we have all made that choice at one time or another. Usually, we have made that choice a lot. We call that sin.

God hates sin, not because He doesn't want us to make our own choices but because He knows more than we do, and if He has warned us about it, it will harm us and others. We may not think so, but we have to admit that the God who created the universe knows more about living than we do. We have a grandson who thinks he should get to eat as much chocolate as he wants. His parents know a bit more about the digestive system than he does. Even though he fusses at them, they limit the chocolate he's allowed to eat for his own good.

God also hates seeing the people He loves in pain. There are some who believe that with so much pain in the world, God must not care. We would argue that the situation is exactly the opposite. Jesus told us that God even notices when a sparrow falls to the ground. God hurts much more than we do over every single pain that every single person has felt for all of history. That's a lot of pain. The worst part is, it's not God who caused the pain. He's warned us clearly not to sin, but we do it anyway.

If we're honest, we will admit that we all have a craving for justice. That's why we are constantly suing one another. Even when the infraction is small, we feel like someone needs to pay. Superhero movies are popular because they resonate with the need inside of us for someone to make the bad guy get what is coming to him. But what happens when the bad guy is us? We've hurt people before. We've gossiped. We've mocked. We've been selfish. We've caused people pain, and God felt it and hated it. So what's a loving God to do?

You know what He did. He came Himself and showed us how to do it right. Jesus showed us how to live without harming anyone. He modeled that we could love even those who hurt us. He taught us to forgive others and put them first. He gave us the example to follow, and then He took the punishment for all of that pain. Why was the cross so brutal? Because mankind has caused a lot of harm.

That's pretty far for God to go, but He didn't stop there. Because sin is what leads to death, Jesus didn't have to be held by death and rose back to life. God's plan was to live with those He loves and who love Him for eternity. The problem is that if we keep acting the way we do when we disobey God, eternity will look just like the way we have made earth look now. God will not allow rape, hatred, prejudice, gossip, arrogance, abuse, greed, sexual immorality, or anything else that harms people to be with us forever because that's not heaven—it's hell. So He gave us His teachings and His Holy Spirit to enable us to act more and more like Jesus. That's what being a Christian is. It's believing that God gets to define sin and that Jesus took the punishment for my sin. Now, with the Holy Spirit's help, I'm going to follow the teachings of Jesus even when it's hard. I'll mess up sometimes, but I talk to God about that too and ask for His help to do better.

The best part is, because I'm letting God help me act more like Jesus, someday I won't have to struggle with it anymore, and I will get to live forever with God and all the others who have wanted to stop sinning. No one will hurt anyone else. No one will be selfish. No one will be greedy. No one will harm nature. No one will abuse anyone. Yes, please!

As Christians, that's what we believe to our very core. That's what your parents believe, and they want to share that beautiful paradise forever with you. The thought that they may not breaks their hearts.

While we are working on acting more like Jesus, we get it wrong sometimes. I promise that your parents, no matter how good their intentions were, got it wrong sometimes. If you were a church kid, you're probably familiar with the Ten Commandments. Those are good rules. Take the Sabbath, for example. How good is God that He wanted to make sure we didn't work ourselves to exhaustion or have others work us to exhaustion. Taking a day to simply rest and spend time with Him is evidence that the one who makes the rules loves us deeply. Did you know that by the time Jesus came to earth, more than thirty-nine categories, with multiple laws in each, had been made to protect the law of the Sabbath? For example, in Israel today there are still Sabbath elevators that will stop at every floor, so you don't have to "work" on the Sabbath by pushing a button.

When we care about God's laws, we have a tendency to want to add our own to them to strengthen or protect them. The Jewish people did that, and Christians do it too. Sometimes we've made rules about dating or

RESTORE THE ROAD HOME

what you should wear. Some of us still argue about which day we should meet on and what we should eat or drink. The motivation is often good, but sometimes we have made rules that God never asked us to. If any of those rules have bothered you, have a conversation with your parents about them. They may have been wrong. You may be wrong. Talk about it.

In closing, we want to ask you to do three things:

1. Forgive Your Parents

Even if your parents were wonderfully loving and supportive, you can probably think of some times that they messed up. They're human, and yeah, they got it wrong sometimes. Forgive them.

2. Take a Fresh Look at Jesus

Read the Gospels (Matthew, Mark, Luke, and John) and see if He is someone you can follow. If you are thinking you have to follow your parents' version of Him, you're following the wrong thing. We hope you have parents who follow Jesus well and can give you wisdom and counsel as you follow Him. But never mistake who you're looking at. Jesus is the standard. However, when you look at Him, you have to look at all of Him. There will be parts of Him that you will love to follow and other parts that will be much harder. We promise that if you follow even the hard parts, it will be so worth it!

3. Forgive the Church

We don't know one person who hasn't been hurt by someone in the church. Just like your parents and just like you, we in the church sometimes forget to act like Jesus and act too much like us. But just like families, the church is a beautiful place with imperfect people who need to be given grace and space to grow and change more and more into the likeness of our Savior.

Before we go, if you have suffered any abuse—verbal, mental, sexual, or physical—by someone claiming to be a follower of Jesus, we are so

125

RESTORE THE ROAD HOME

sorry. The Bible warns us clearly that there will be people who say they follow Jesus but in reality are wolves who selfishly desire to harm others. A true follower of Jesus will mess up sometimes, but their life should be characterized by loving, serving, and giving up what they want for others. If the example you have seen was selfish, cruel, and demanding, that person is not a follower of Jesus. They are an impostor. We want to assure you that there are true Christians out there who would love to help bring healing to those areas in which you have suffered. Keep looking until you find them, and ask God to help you. He will—we promise!

CHAPTER 12

SCRIPTURES TO PRAY

I n chapter 5 we talked about the power of speaking God's Word back to Him. Here, we have given you twenty Scriptures you can pray and an example prayer for each topic. Feel free to pick and choose, depending on what you or your child is going through right now. Or you can go through them in order and pray one each day.

ANXIETY

Scripture

1 Peter 5:5–7
"'God opposes the proud but shows favor to the humble.' Humble yourselves, therefore, under God's mighty hand, that he may lift you up in due time. Cast all your anxiety on him because he cares for you."

Prayer

Father, your Word says that you oppose the proud but show favor to the humble. Help me to walk in humility before you and others. I submit to your plans and timing and trust that in your timing, not mine, you will answer my prayers. Thank you that I can cast my worries on you, so I throw (name the things making you anxious) on you. I will leave these things in your loving hands. Thank you that you care so much for me that you willingly carry my burdens, so I don't have to spend the day worrying about them.

Declarations

God's timing is better than mine.

I have nothing to worry about because God will show me favor.

My anxieties have been thrown on God. He is faithful to carry them, so I will not pick them up again.

BITTERNESS

Scripture

Ephesians 4:31–32
"Get rid of all bitterness, rage and anger, brawling and slander, along with every form of malice. Be kind and compassionate to one another, forgiving each other, just as in Christ God forgave you."

Hebrews 12:15
"See to it that no one falls short of the grace of God and that no bitter root grows up to cause trouble and defile many."

Prayer

Father, your Word is clear that I am not allowed to hold on to any kind of bitterness, rage, anger, or unforgiveness and all the things that come with them. I know that those things don't only affect me, but they can spread and defile many others. Help me to have no part of that. With your help, God, I will not harbor any bitterness toward (name/s). If I have slandered or caused any damage, please forgive me.

Declarations

Bitterness, rage, and anger will have no place in my heart.

Today I let go of even the slightest bit of bitterness I may have toward (name/s).

I will not slander or react in rage toward anyone today. I will clothe myself in Christ.

CONFUSION

Scripture

John 13:7
"Jesus replied, 'You do not realize now what I am doing, but later you will understand.'"

Prayer

Lord, I know that I do not see the whole picture and you do. Your ways are too big for me, and I cannot even begin to fathom all that you think and do. I will trust you even though I don't understand because my faith rests on who you are, not on what I think you should do.

Declarations

Jesus is much smarter than I am.

It's silly to think that I will always understand what He does and why.

I will trust my Lord in all circumstances.

DISCOURAGEMENT

Scripture

Isaiah 59:1
"Surely the arm of the Lord is not too short to save, nor his ear too dull to hear."

Prayer

*Father, I have been praying so long for salvation for those I love. Help me not to get discouraged but to keep on fighting hard because I **know** that your arm is not too short to save. I **know** that you hear me. I trust your wisdom and timing. You know more than I do, and you love them more than I do.*

Declarations

God is mighty and can save the hardest of hearts.

God is all-knowing and opens people's eyes when the timing is right.

God loves (name/s) so much bigger than I do.

FEAR

Scripture

Luke 10:19–20
"I have given you authority to trample on snakes and scorpions and to overcome all the power of the enemy; nothing will harm you. However, do not rejoice that the spirits submit to you, but rejoice that your names are written in heaven."

Prayer

Lord Jesus, what a privilege and blessing it is to walk in all of the authority you have given me. Thank you for allowing me to function in your power.

I will not fear (name what you are tempted to be fearful of)! I overpower any spirit attempting to cause chaos, fear, or pain in this area in the name of Jesus. Thank you, Lord, that nothing can harm me, and I will be with you for eternity.

Declarations

I have been given power and authority from Jesus Himself.

Nothing will harm me because my Savior is attentive to me.

My name is written in the Lamb's Book of Life. I am safe for eternity!

FORGIVENESS

Scripture

Colossians 3:12–14
"Therefore, as God's chosen people, holy and dearly loved, clothe yourselves with compassion, kindness, humility, gentleness and patience. Bear with each other and forgive one another if any of you has a grievance against someone. Forgive as the Lord forgave you. And over all these virtues put on love, which binds them all together in perfect unity."

Prayer

Father, I am amazed by your great love for me. Thank you that your Word tells me that I am dearly loved by you. Sometimes I struggle to be compassionate, kind, humble, gentle, and patient, especially when someone hurts me. Help me, by the power of your Holy Spirit, to be clothed in those things today. I remember how you have forgiven me, so I forgive (name/s). In light of your love for me, enable me to love (name/s).

Declarations

I am so dearly loved by God.

With God's help, I will treat people with compassion, kindness, humility, gentleness, and patience today.

I have forgiven (name/s) for (offense), and I will not keep dwelling on it.

GRIEF

Scripture

Isaiah 61:3
"To bestow on them a crown of beauty instead of ashes, the oil of joy instead of mourning, and a garment of praise instead of a spirit of despair. They will be called oaks of righteousness, a planting of the Lord for the display of his splendor."

Prayer

What a great God you are that you are not afraid of ashes. Dead or destroyed things do not turn you away. This situation seems hopeless to me, but I serve the God who can even make something beautiful from ashes! Please take this situation and bring life, beauty, and joy to it. I shake off my despair and give you the praise you so richly deserve.

Declarations

My God can take this ugly thing I'm going through and make something beautiful from it.

I will take the oil of joy from my Father because I know what He is capable of.

Not only will beauty come from these ashes, but that beauty will display the Lord's splendor.

NEGATIVE THOUGHTS

Scripture

Philippians 4:4–9
"Rejoice in the Lord always. I will say it again: Rejoice! Let your gentleness be evident to all. The Lord is near. Do not be anxious about anything, but in every situation, by prayer and petition, with thanksgiving, present your requests to God. And the peace of God, which transcends all understanding, will guard your hearts and your minds in Christ Jesus. Finally, brothers and sisters, whatever is true, whatever is noble, whatever is right, whatever is pure, whatever is lovely, whatever is admirable—if anything is excellent or praiseworthy—think about such things. Whatever you have learned or received or heard from me, or seen in me—put it into practice. And the God of peace will be with you."

2 Corinthians 10:5
"We demolish arguments and every pretension that sets itself up against the knowledge of God, and we take captive every thought to make it obedient to Christ."

Prayer

Lord, I know that my words and actions flow from the thoughts that are in my head. I'm having a hard time with those thoughts right now. My mind wants to spiral into all of the what-ifs, fears, and hurts. I stop that spiral now, in Jesus's name. I arrest thoughts that do not line up with your Word and make them submit to you. Here are my requests (name them). I present them to you. I align my thoughts to what is true. That means that first of all, I rejoice in your goodness today. You are great, holy, kind, and generous. I will trust you in every situation because you are faithful. I will not only stop the negative thoughts, but I will replace them with the things my mind should be dwelling on. Help me to see what is noble, right, pure, lovely, admirable, excellent, and praiseworthy. Help me to put your Word into practice so that I may walk in peace.

Declarations

I have every reason to rejoice today because I have God, and He is all I need to have joy.

I have given my requests to God, and I can trust Him with my fears and desires.

When a negative thought tries to rear its ugly head, I will capture it and replace it with the truth of God's Word.

PEACE

John 16:33
"I have told you these things, so that in me you may have peace. In this world you will have trouble. But take heart! I have overcome the world."

Prayer

Your Word is clear, Lord, that this world will give us troubles. Yet there is always peace in you. When my heart is in turmoil, remind me that your desire is for me to walk in peace and that peace does not rest on my circumstances. It rests on you alone. Thank you that you have overcome this wicked world, and you give me your peace to walk through it.

Declarations

I will not be surprised when this world brings me trouble. My Savior has already forewarned me.

I will not allow my circumstances to rob me of my peace.

My peace rests in Jesus alone, and He will never leave me or forsake me.

I will attach my peace to Jesus and not to the outcome of the circumstances around me.

RECONCILIATION

Scripture

2 Corinthians 5:17–20
"Therefore, if anyone is in Christ, the new creation has come: The old has gone, the new is here! All this is from God, who reconciled us to himself through Christ and gave us the ministry of reconciliation: that God was reconciling the world to himself in Christ, not counting people's sins against them. And he has committed to us the message of reconciliation. We are therefore Christ's ambassadors, as though God were making his appeal through us. We implore you on Christ's behalf: Be reconciled to God."

Prayer

Thank you, Lord, that I am new, changed, and different because you have made me that way. Thank you that I no longer act and react the way I used to before I knew you. Where my old ways of acting have caused damage, please help me to repair it. Help me to show others how to become a new creation in Christ. Help me to reconcile people to you and to be someone who helps bring restoration to broken relationships. Your Word says that I am your ambassador and you have given me this job. Enable me to do it in the power of your Holy Spirit.

Declarations

Because I am in Christ, I act and react to circumstances like Jesus, not like I used to.

God has reconciled me to Himself and does not count my sins against me.

Today I will make being God's ambassador my number one priority. I will look for ways to reconcile people to God and bring healing to broken relationships.

SHAME

Scripture

Romans 10:11
"As Scripture says, 'Anyone who believes in him will never be put to shame.'"

Romans 8:1
"Therefore, there is now no condemnation for those who are in Christ Jesus."

Prayer

Father, thank you that I don't have to walk in the shame of my past, my mistakes, or my failures. Help me to remember that I am righteous, holy, cleansed, and forgiven, and I have a purpose because of the blood of Jesus. Please remove every ounce of shame from my mind, and enable me to look more like Jesus today than I did yesterday.

Declarations

I am free, holy, clean, and forgiven in the sight of God Almighty.

I will not take back the shame or condemnation that God has removed.

I will ask for the Holy Spirit's help to make my actions and thoughts align with my Savior's.

SPIRITUAL WARFARE

Scripture

Ephesians 6:10–13
"Finally, be strong in the Lord and in his mighty power. Put on the full armor of God, so that you can take your stand against the devil's schemes. For our struggle is not against flesh and blood, but against the rulers, against the authorities, against the powers of this dark world and against the spiritual forces of evil in the heavenly realms. Therefore put on the full armor of God, so that when the day of evil comes, you may be able to stand your ground, and after you have done everything, to stand."

2 Corinthians 10:4
"The weapons we fight with are not the weapons of the world. On the contrary, they have divine power to demolish strongholds."

Prayer

Heavenly Father, thank you that you lend your might and power to me, and I am able to fight battles and win victories for your kingdom. I recognize that I do not fight against any person, but I do battle against any spirit that would set itself against you and your kingdom. I demolish every stronghold in my life and in my child's life in the mighty name of Jesus. Holy Spirit, please give me discernment to see where the battle is and the strength to stand against the enemy.

Declarations

My child, my spouse, my parents, or any other person is not my enemy. Satan is my enemy, and I will direct my attacks at him.

The battles I fight are fought in the strength and power of my Lord, Jesus Christ, and I fight from a place of victory through Him.

I will arm myself each day with the truth of God's Word so that I can stand against my enemy.

STRENGTH

Scripture

Isaiah 40:31
"But those who hope in the Lord will renew their strength. They will soar on wings like eagles; they will run and not grow weary, they will walk and not be faint."

Prayer

Father, I need your strength today. The circumstances around me can sometimes cause me to feel overwhelmed and wonder if I will have the stamina to go on. But today I am putting my hope in you. I do not hope in my finances, my friends, my circumstances, my job, my family, my status, my ministry, my accomplishments, or my reputation. I put my hope in you alone. Because my hope is attached where it should be, your Word tells me that I will have the strength and energy to accomplish all that you have planned for me today. Help me to remember that I don't have to do any more than that.

Declarations

I will put my hope only in the Lord today.

I will have all of the energy and strength I need to run and soar today.

I do not have to do any more than God has planned for me.

UNDER ATTACK

Scripture

Psalm 28:6–7
"Praise be to the Lord, for he has heard my cry for mercy. The Lord is my strength and my shield; my heart trusts in him, and he helps me."

Prayer

Father, my circumstances are scaring me, and I'm feeling like so many are against me. Help me to walk according to your Word. As I am obedient to you, thank you that you are my strength and my shield. I trust you in this situation.

Declarations

I do not need to carry the stress of defending myself.

The Lord is the one who strengthens and shields me.

Even when I would do it differently, I will trust Him to be my defender.

WEAKNESS

Scripture

2 Corinthians 12:9–10
"But he said to me, 'My grace is sufficient for you, for my power is made perfect in weakness.' Therefore I will boast all the more gladly about my weaknesses, so that Christ's power may rest on me. That is why, for Christ's sake, I delight in weaknesses, in insults, in hardships, in persecutions, in difficulties. For when I am weak, then I am strong."

Prayer

What a relief, Lord, that you do not depend on my strength. I simply don't have enough strength, wisdom, stamina, or even love to navigate all that life throws at me. What an amazing God you are that my weakness does not turn you away but actually makes your power even more perfect because it comes completely from you. Help me to delight in my weaknesses and see your power moving.

Declarations

My weaknesses do not turn God away from me.

The things that God has put on my heart do not depend on my strength but on His.

I will thank God that my weaknesses make room for Him to get all of the glory when He uses me to do mighty things for His kingdom.

WISDOM

Scripture

James 1:5–6
"If any of you lacks wisdom, you should ask God, who gives generously to all without finding fault, and it will be given to you. But when you ask, you must believe and not doubt, because the one who doubts is like a wave of the sea, blown and tossed by the wind."

Prayer

I don't know what to do in this situation, Father, but I praise you that you do. You understand the things that confuse me and that are hidden from me. Please give me wisdom. It's true that I have faults, but how amazing that your Word tells me that you will give me wisdom generously, without finding any fault in me, because I am yours through Jesus Christ.

Declarations

I don't have to figure things out on my own.

I will ask God for the wisdom I need to navigate confusing or painful situations.

I will not be timid when I come to God and ask for wisdom, because He does not find fault with me.

CHAPTER 13

STORIES OF HOPE

To say I was once a prodigal is a completely accurate statement. I was once so far away from the Lord and just living for myself and my selfish ambitions.

I grew up in church my whole life. My grandparents and parents are very strong in their relationship with the Lord. Their godly heritage and continued prayers would one day shape my future and prepare the way for my great hunger and desperation for Yeshua. It would break the veil for me to see who I am and Whose I am.

As a young teenager I got into groups of the wrong friends. I was seeking acceptance and self-worth in other people. I dabbled in witchcraft, got into meth and drinking, and slept with boys out of wedlock. I was lost. At seventeen years old I got pregnant. I immediately knew I had to sober up. The young man that got me pregnant begged me to abort. But in my heart, I knew that was wrong. We ended up going our separate ways, and I had a little girl.

I was a single parent living with my parents. When I told my parents I was pregnant, they went through a lot of different emotions. They never broke relationship with me. They came alongside me and helped me. They also continued to pray for me. After hopping around from guy to guy, I'd had enough. I drew a line in the sand and decided I wanted to settle down and have a family. That's when I met my wonderful husband. He had two children, an ex-wife, and baggage. He didn't follow the Lord or even know about Jesus. At this time I was twenty-one.

We got married two years later. It was a hard road to say the least. We would fight hard, throw things, and just be horrible to each other. I was constantly calling my mom and crying to her. She would always give me godly counsel and advice. My marriage was failing. I blamed my husband a lot. I wanted him to change. I had fifty different false expectations in my marriage. I ended up moving out, and my husband and I separated. He wanted a divorce.

It was in this hour I began praying to God. I was desperate. I was desperate for God to change ME. For months I would go to work, pick up my daughter, and then go home and pray. I prayed for healing and restoration in my broken marriage and with my children. My parents were praying for me and my family. My grandparents were praying for me and my family.

Then, on our court date to finalize our divorce, my husband changed his mind. God moved. God showed Himself. We decided to work hard to change our old habits. We decided to make God FIRST in our marriage. God wasn't done with me yet. During the next few years we did a lot of changing. We had a whole new appreciation for each other. We appreciated the Lord for giving us a second chance.

And then, when I was thirty-three years old, I became so bored with the day-to-day life. I thought, "Is this all there is?" So I started a war room in my house. I had an extra bedroom and spent every morning there in prayer. I would pray for people at our church, pray for my children, read the Bible, and just talk to the Lord. I was desperate again! You see, during my life I still went to church, I just had no relationship with Jesus. In fact, I couldn't even raise my hands in worship. Worship at church always made me uncomfortable. But I knew there had to be more.

Jeremiah 29:13 says, "You will seek me and find me when you seek me with all your heart." So that's what I did.

Then Jesus did it again. One day I was praying on the couch, and all of a sudden this electrifying power came over me. I immediately raised my hands. I could not stop. I was shaking and crying uncontrollably. I called my mom, and I remember her happy-crying and saying, "That's the Holy Spirit." From that day forward, God would transform not only my husband's and my lives, but us. I became addicted to Jesus. I wanted nothing more than to spend time with my Lord. I was baptized in Holy Spirit fire and ready for more. Holy Spirit started waking me up every night around 3:00 a.m. just to spend time together. This in itself was pretty incredible since I took medication to sleep at night. I would get up and go in my war room, worship with my hands held high, and pray. This became our routine. Then one night I heard Him speak. He would tell me things about people that would be dear to their hearts. I would write out letters to people from Jesus. I got to see visions and feel feelings for the people I was writing to, but through Christ's eyes. I witnessed people crying as they read these letters. I heard some say, "How could you have known that?"

This season of my life became a snowball of miraculous events. Every time God would show up, it left me humbled and in awe of His mighty power and who He is. My husband got to experience this with me. He became a worshiper too! Today, we have a healthy, loving marriage of eighteen years and have been together for twenty years. My husband is so precious to me. I give all the glory to my first love, Jesus. He is the absolute lover of my soul. The one I cherish, the one I adore, and I'm completely in love with Him.

You see, my friend, if it had not been for my praying grandparents or my praying parents, where would I be? Lost, empty, hurting. But they did. God heard their prayers and intervened.

Now I have three children who do not follow the Lord. They don't know His heart, His nature, His character, HIM. One of our children lives a homosexual lifestyle. So now I am the one on my knees crying out to God, "Please save my prodigals!"

My story isn't over. In fact, if there is breath in my lungs, it is still being written. And guess what, I am desperate for Him again.

GRACE'S STORY

I grew up a typical pastor's kid. Late Saturday nights and all-day Sundays spent running around my parents' church, hiding in the offices, running through the chairs in the sanctuary, and playing with friends. It wasn't until I hit junior high that I realized my life looked a little different from the rest of my peers. I wasn't allowed to do a lot of things they were. Staying out late, parties, having boyfriends, etc. This caught my attention and steered me in the wrong direction. I soon found myself lost in the things of this world. Dating non-Christian boys, sneaking out late at night, partying, and alcohol quickly consumed me. After some years of chasing the wrong things and coming up feeling incredibly empty and purposeless, somehow my heart cracked open, and He finally got my attention. It was a Sunday in September of 2012 when it all changed for me. I was sitting in the front row with my parents at church when a flood of tears took over me. I had a moment of clarity that I had been ignoring for some time. It had been a conversation after my high school graduation about what I wanted to do next. Bible college was an option, but it always went in one ear and out the other for me. My heart has always been sensitive in the worship moments at church, and it was in this setting that the Lord grabbed hold of me. I knew what God wanted me to do. I leaned over to them and said "I know what I need to do. I want to go to Bible college."

January of 2013, my nineteen-year-old self said goodbye to friends and family and moved across the world to attend Bible college in Sydney, Australia. The Lord quickly took over my heart and my life, and I've never looked back. I spent three years there immersed in church life, ministry, leadership classes, and friendships that would last a lifetime. I met my husband there and all our best friends who we still do life with to this day. I had a complete transformation overnight. He gave me a new heart and put a new spirit within me. He took my heart of stone and gave me a heart of flesh (Ezekiel 36:26). The Lord has been faithful all the days of my life. He's never failed me. His goodness, grace, and mercy were upon me in every moment, even when I didn't know it or understand it. All the years my parents spent pleading with the Lord for my life had come to fruition. As a mother now to two beautiful girls myself, it's the only thing I could ever ask from the Lord. That He be as faithful and merciful to them as He has been to me. That they never turn away from Him. If I could encourage any parents who are praying for their child to come to know the Lord, I would say, never give up on your children, no matter how hopeless it might seem. It wasn't one giant magical moment for me. It was little by little, subtle whispers from the Holy Spirit, years of prayerful parents, and one faithful God. My life and my world have forever been marked by the power and steadfast love of Jesus.

KAREN'S STORY

Our son was sitting outside at the side of our home after we had told him that he had to leave by midnight that night. We had spent years doing everything we knew to do to help him: prayer, drug counseling, a year in Teen Challenge—to no avail. He told us that he had no place to go and he wasn't going to leave.

My husband went outside and told him, "Son, your mom and I have been married a long time, and this is putting a wedge in our marriage, as we are not on the same page." I was convinced that tough love was needed. With that statement our son said to his father, "I've messed up my life, but I don't want to mess up your marriage. I will be out of here by midnight tonight." With that he went out into the night. He was twenty years old.

The one thing about young rebellious kids is they will find other kids, other families to live with to figure it out until they can go on their own. He had a great work ethic, which helped him find work and grow up while still doing his addictions. We knew he could not come home with all of his addictions, because there were two younger sisters in the home that were not getting the attention they needed because he had drained us emotionally.

He remained struggling all those years, until . . .

Close to his thirty-third birthday, I felt the Lord speak to my heart to bring him back home. I didn't want to do it, but when I came home from work that day, I shared with my husband what I felt I heard the Lord say. My husband said the Lord had spoken to him a couple weeks before, and he was just waiting for the Lord to speak to me. We then invited him to come home. He arrived with all of his addictions, but there was a gentler side of him coming through the door.

On the night before his birthday I spoke these words to him, "Son, the Lord Jesus died in the thirty-third year of his life. What if you began to live in this new thirty-third year of your life?" and with that my husband and I went to our bedroom. Later that evening, prior to midnight, we had a knock on our door, and our son came in and said, "Mom and Dad, will you bless me?" You've never seen two parents jump out of bed so fast. We laid hands on him and we blessed him.

That night, after asking forgiveness and repenting of his sins to the Lord Jesus, he went out to the street and threw his pornography, tobacco, drugs, and alcohol into the drain. He returned home and slept unassisted for the first time in many, many years. When he awoke the next morning, he knew the Lord had miraculously delivered him of those four addictions.

He wanted to first speak to our pastor to share what had happened. He also went to a group of women that met every Sunday after church to pray for the prodigals in our church. Aware they had been praying for him, he shared his victory and thanked them. Later that week he shared with his father and me what had happened the night before his thirty-third birthday.

To this day he drinks alcohol when socially appropriate but never out of control. None of the other addictions have been in his world again. This summer, at age forty-five, he just got married to a most beautiful lady. For years their dates were long walks as they got to know each other. He knows and loves her family as she loves his.

God is faithful! Never stop praying! We have not because we ask not. Finally, God's timing is always perfect.

DIANA'S STORY

I grew up in a loving Christian home. Church and following Jesus was the foundation of our family. For as long as I can remember, everyone in my world knew that I was a Christian. Every summer as a child, I would invite my friends at school to VBS. As I got older, the invitations changed to youth group. I was the church girl. If the kids on the playground said a bad word and happened to see me standing nearby, they would always apologize. That kind of bothered me.

After I graduated from high school, I went on a month-long trip across the country. When I returned, the church I had attended for years had dissolved. My youth group no longer existed, and the friends I had there had all gone in different directions. We were still friends, but we were no longer a unit and no longer had spiritual leadership.

I got a job and started attending the local junior college. I began making new friends. These friends didn't know anything about me. These friends didn't apologize for cussing in front of me. It dawned on me that I didn't have to be different anymore. I could be just like them and be included in all the things they did if I just wasn't a Christian. So I began to embrace the things they did and reject the faith I had grown up in. At first, it felt amazing to throw off those shackles of religion and do whatever I wanted. One day while I was at the beach drinking with friends, I saw two of the most popular girls from my high school. They were delighted with my newfound "freedom" and told me, "If we had known that you partied, we would have hung out with you more." Wow! That was all it took to be accepted into the "in" crowd? Sign me up!

Everything was fun, at first. However, I slowly began to notice things about myself I didn't like. I was more anxious than I used to be. I always worried that I was being left out of something. I was certainly more promiscuous and self-centered. I could see myself hardening. I didn't like it, but I didn't know what to do about it.

The obvious answer would have been to return to Christ. The problem with that was that I had some issues with God. During my wandering from Him, I had allowed myself to give full vent to some of the things that had always bothered me. Why couldn't I hear Him speak to me? Why was there so much suffering if He was good? Why couldn't I understand the Bible? To be honest, I was mad at God because I didn't believe He had been all He was cracked up to be.

My parents were concerned. They were praying and struggling to know what to do. One day my mom invited me to try out a new church with her. I was not excited about that. She knew the way to coerce me to do anything was to offer new clothes. She told me she would buy me a new dress if I went. After a shopping trip to the mall, off to church we went! The church was putting on an Easter production that evening. My mom wanted to go. Since there were some cute guys in the church, I agreed to go with her. I was not expecting what happened next.

The play was exactly what you would expect from a church with a small budget. Since I knew the story well and the acting left a lot to be desired, I knew this cheesy performance would have no effect on me. Then they got to the scene where the soldiers were nailing Jesus to the cross. With every hammer blow, I felt my heart breaking. I wanted to cry, but my mom was sitting right next to me, and I couldn't let her think that this

RESTORE THE ROAD HOME

thing was getting to me. I thought about running out of the church, but that wouldn't work either. I clenched my fists, ground my teeth, and forced those tears back. That was a close one, and I was happy to get out of that place and back home.

I needed to focus on something else, so after my parents went to bed, I popped in a movie, *Return of the Jedi*. Just before the scene where Luke saves his father, I heard the Lord speak to my heart, "Turn the movie off. I want to talk to you." I can't even tell you how I knew it was God. I just did. I argued back and told Him the movie was almost over and we would talk then. God spoke to my heart again and said, "Why should I still be here when the movie is over?" For the first time, I felt scared because I knew I didn't deserve the attention of God. What if this was my last chance for relationship with Him? I turned off the movie and got my Bible.

I waited for the Lord to speak again. What did He want to say? Where should I read? Nothing but silence. I got mad. I said to the Lord, "Isn't this what you always do? I want to hear you speak, and you don't say a word." I decided I would take matters into my own hands and just start at the beginning of the New Testament. I turned to Matthew. I saw "Matthew" at the top of the page. I began to read. This wasn't Matthew! Where were the genealogies? Where was the birth of Christ? I had never read these words before. This was God giving a rebuke to people who had taken Him for granted and spoken things about Him that weren't true. I looked back to the top of the page, and it said "Malachi."

I sobbed as I read the entire book of Malachi and saw myself in these hard-hearted people. I asked the Lord to forgive me for being just like them and to cleanse my sins through the blood of Jesus. I have never been the same. Scripture came alive to me after that! I couldn't get enough of it and kept thinking, "Has this always been in here?" I completely fell in love with my Savior, and I continually thank Him for the grace and mercy He gave me that night.

I call that night my "Malachi moment." Now I have my own adult children who have walked away from the God who loves them so dearly. As I write this, I am praying they, as well as your children, have a Malachi moment of their own, where the Lord speaks directly to their hearts and draws them back to Him.

REID'S STORY

Excerpts from a letter that Reid asked his mom to share with her prayer group:

Dear Prayer Warriors,

I want to begin by thanking each and every one of you. Your endless prayers have not gone unheard, and the support you have given my family and me means the absolute world to me.

The last few months, I had been in one of the lowest lows of my entire life. I kept telling myself "tomorrow." I was living without purpose. I had no job, no desire to do anything, and I just kept making excuses. Whatever it was, I was really struggling.

Well, God heard my prayers and knew my heart. He showed me another way out, and I say this with absolute certainty: this is where I am supposed to be. Within one week, I was inspired to pack my things and move to Fresno. I have been here about a month now, and the Lord has spoken to me more times than ever in my life. Before now, I could count only a few times when I've experienced a true interaction with God. Now He has appeared so vividly, He might as well have been waving His hands in my face and screaming, "I'm here, Reid!"

Before I moved I was dealing with heartbreak. I was hurting a lot more than I let on. I prayed and prayed for a way out, and when I got the opportunity to leave, I took it. And I have gotten freaking blessed. Psalm 23, my cup overflows. It's like my wildest dreams came true. I still can't even believe it because every day something new happens, and it just gets better and better.

This last week or so was REALLY rough for me. I was alone. Doubt was circulating, as well as residue from my breakup. Never in my life have I fought a battle every day so hard in my head. Instead of moping around and feeling sad, I was proactive—praying, working out, walking, listening to inspirational videos, you name it.

April 23, 2023, is a day I will remember for the rest of my life. What was supposed to be a chill day turned into more than a two-hour walk on a dirt road that led to absolutely nowhere. I can't make you see or feel what was in my mind, but I was going through it. Ugly-crying as bad as it gets as I walked this seemingly endless road, no one around for miles. Just me battling my demons. At some point along that road, I decided that I had had enough. I decided that I was going to change my life, and all that BS from the past was not going to have control of me anymore. I was flooded with emotion beyond anything I have felt before. And I know this might sound crazy. In that moment, I was so in my mind, so intense, it felt as if this evil presence stirring inside of me was slowly being ripped out of my chest until finally I exhaled and I was free. If that wasn't crazy enough, it was then, clear as the sky is blue, that God was walking right there with me. Right there on the road, no one around for miles, He was there in all white.

These last few nights I've tossed and turned, just knowing in my heart that I wanted to send this message to you all. I truly believe it is because of your endless prayers that every star has now aligned in my life. This is not to say that I'm good to coast on, and everything will now be OK. This is not going to be easy. After experiencing what I've gone through this last month, I'm prepared for absolutely anything.

Now is where I ask for your help. I need you all to come together and pray for me as if I am sitting in the very center of your circle tonight. Pray for my heart, my courage, my resilience, my will to be the man God wants me to be. I know He bestowed something greater in me. Pray that I continue living the words that I speak and find my way. I want to thank you all for letting me share, and again, your love for me has quite literally changed my life.

Love,
Reid

CONCLUSION

We hope these stories encouraged you. You serve a God who is constantly working in ways we cannot always see. Trust Him with those children you hold so dear.

As we come to the end of our book, we want to invite you to continue the journey with us at our website:

R3-ministries.com

Here you will be able to share your own stories of hope, ask for prayer and join a community of parents battling together for those the enemy has taken captive. We will be victorious by the power and might of our risen Savior!

WE WOULD LIKE TO THANK

Our precious family: Jordan, Haley, Wesley, Tori, Sebastian & Eloise. You are each a delight and you continually teach us new things.

Chris Sonksen: You encouraged us to write a book and were so patient and honest as we sent you each chapter. You look for the best in people and want to see everyone succeed in their God given gifts. The way you build people up is a gift to the Church.

Our Prayer Team: You have prayed so many prayers for us and this book.

Wayne, Lynn, Carolyn, Andy & Gail: Not only have you prayed for us and with us but you have walked with us through hard things and always given generously of your wisdom.

All of our Battle Cry friends: You have held our hearts, let us be vulnerable, carried our burdens and let us carry yours. We have been a safe place for each other and that is worth more than gold.

Mosaic Church: You beautiful church! How we love you and thank you for the love you show us.

Dawn Gutierrez: Thank you for believing in us and the message of this book.

Robin Reed: Your edits, expertise and encouragement were such a blessing to us.

Scott Allan: Thank you for guiding us through the publishing process.

Finally, simple words of thanks to our Lord Jesus will never be enough. We hope this entire book, and our entire lives, express our gratitude and devotion to the One who gave everything for us!

BIBLIOGRAPHY

Smalley, Gary and Trent, John. *The Blessing*. Pocket Books. 1990.

Bailey, Kenneth E. *The Cross and the Prodigal*. IVP. 2005.

Moore, Beth. *Chasing Vines*. Tyndale Momentum. 2020.

Terkeurst, Lysa. *It's Not Supposed to be This Way*. Thomas Nelson. 2018.

Ten Boom, Corrie. *The Hiding Place*. Chosen Books. 1971.

Wolf, Katherine and Jay. *Hope Heals*. Zondervan. 2020.

Deal, Ron L. *The Smart Step Family*. Bethany House Publishers. 2014.

Wonder Woman. Jenkins, Patty. Warner Brothers. 2017.

Rocky IV. Stallone, Sylvester. United Artists Chartoff-Winkler Productions. 1985.

Creed II. Caple, Steven Jr. Metro Goldwyn-Mayer Pictures and Warner Brothers. 2018.

ABOUT THE AUTHORS

Jeff and Diana Seaman have been serving in ministry for over 30 years. For 15 years, Jeff was a pastor at KLOVE Radio where he navigated people from across the world through life's spiritual and emotional challenges. They currently pastor Mosaic Christian Church in Rocklin, CA and founded R3 Ministries. The goal of R3 Ministries is to rebuild, repair and restore lives and relationships that are in ruins (Isaiah 58:11-14). They love hiking, good food, painting, puzzling and being bossed around by their grandchildren.

Made in the USA
Columbia, SC
02 June 2024

dc10c920-0cdf-4bb4-acf5-680fdd3a6368R01